ADVANCE PRAISE

"Blue-collar entrepreneurs are near and dear to my heart. Kenny's passion and skillset are second to none. If you are a blue-collar entrepreneur, this book is a must-read!"

—**GINO WICKMAN**, author of Traction and Entrepreneurial Leap

"Wow! Just wow! I've long been a Kenny Chapman fan. This book blew me away. All of us have dark places that lurk beneath our shiny, glossy, polished exteriors. Kenny shares some of his. He also addresses the real issues business owners face, or rather, avoid. The goal of business ownership is to build a business that works for you, not the reverse. Not only has Kenny done it, but he takes you on the journey to discovering a personal higher purpose that will enable, if not compel, you to do the same. If you're a business owner or leader, read this book. If you're the spouse of a business owner or leader, buy the book for your spouse."

—**MATT MICHEL**, Founder and President of Service Nation Inc.

"I knew even before I opened this book that it would be a great read. I wasn't disappointed. It lays out leadership principles that are easy to follow and understand, even for the newest manager. I am going to purchase the book for all the leaders in the organization and make it required reading. Well done, Kenny, and thank you!"

—**ALAN O'NEILL**, CEO and Founder at Abacus Plumbing and CEO at the Wrench Group South Central Region

"Kenny nailed it. This book is incredibly clear. The message is easily relatable to my personal struggles. As I read the book, I felt like Kenny was speaking directly to me. The book helped me see a clear path to being free from all of the mental traps that I have held on to for years! I am more excited today than ever about my incredible future! Thank you, Kenny!"

—**KEITH JACKSON**, Owner and Manager of Jackson Plumbing Heating and Cooling

"I met Kenny a few years ago and have been impressed with his ability to communicate and share his knowledge. He does so in a way that helps contractors produce a much more powerful team in their business and empower and grow their leaders. This book exemplifies living a good life as an owner. It's what we aspired to do the day we opened our businesses."

—**MICHAEL BREWER**, CEO of Ben Franklin Plumbing AZ and The Brewer Companies

"Kenny's book is extremely well done. I knew from the beginning this was the right book for me. The book is easy to read and contains such great information that helps my team improve communication immediately. Thank you, Kenny!"

—**TOMMY MELLO**, Owner/Operator at A1 Garage Door Service, author of Home Service Millionaire, and host of Home Service Expert Podcast

"In this book, Kenny shares his success path as a contractor. He has been where you are and has written a book that shows you his time-tested best way forward. If you're willing to change your mindset about what is possible in your contracting business and your life, this book is an absolute must for you!"

—**AL LEVI**, The 7-Power Contractor

"In this book, Kenny shares relatable information and insights while walking us through clear, understandable steps that have helped not only me but our entire team become better. I have renewed excitement and a pathway for how my business success can support and even complement my personal life as well as my entire team!"

—**JANEEN NORQUIST**, Co-Owner and President of Just in Time Heating, AC, Plumbing & Remodeling

"Here's a no-nonsense problem to solve: Kenny's wisdom on paper + your eyes + action = your life improved × 10."

—**MIKE NICOLAI**, President of Triton Air

BLUE COLLAR
COLLAR
SUCCESS LAWS

BLUE COLLAR
SUCCESS LAWS

Your No-Nonsense Guide to Problem-Solving, Productivity, & Profit

KENNY CHAPMAN

COPYRIGHT © 2022 KENNY CHAPMAN

All rights reserved.

BLUE COLLAR SUCCESS LAWS

Your No-Nonsense Guide to Problem-Solving, Productivity, & Profit

ISBN	978-1-5445-3167-0	*Hardcover*
	978-1-5445-3166-3	*Paperback*
	978-1-5445-3168-7	*Ebook*

This book would not have been possible without my own personal decision and commitment to face my pain and suffering head-on and to go through the life-changing process of addiction recovery. I'm grateful to Gordie Bufton for introducing me to David Essel who helped me immensely in turning a very dark and painful life situation into an amazing awakening like never before, filled with love, joy, and bliss daily in this incredibly wonderful experience we call life.

CONTENTS

Ch 1: Holding You Back and Pushing You to the Brink 1

Ch 2: When the Right Path Is the Wrong Road 13

Ch 3: Purposely Putting the Insanity behind You 23

Ch 4: Law #1 Authentic Abundance 31

Ch 5: Law #2 Relationships before Results 41

Ch 6: Law #3 Problems Hold Solutions 51

Ch 7: Law #4 Purpose-Guided Responsibility 61

Ch 8: Law #5 Candid Communication 73

Ch 9: Law #6 Aligned Accountability 83

Ch 10: Law #7 Essential Self-Care 95

Ch 11: Implementing the 7 Laws 109

Acknowledgments 119

Are You a Service Contractor?
Kenny Founded this Company for You! 121

Additional Books by the Author 123

About the Author 125

CHAPTER 1

HOLDING YOU BACK AND PUSHING YOU TO THE BRINK

I WAS THIRTY YEARS OLD, made tons of money, lived in my dream house, traveled to far-flung destinations, had fancy cars and a luxury motor home, golfed five days a week, and owned a phenomenally successful plumbing/HVAC business that practically ran on autopilot. I only worked when I wanted to and otherwise did as I pleased. I had it all, the American dream, a lifestyle that others spend decades attempting to achieve, and I had accomplished it while still in my prime. With all of that success, everything that anyone could want, I stood on a cliff at the Colorado National Monument and imagined stepping into the abyss.

I was ready to call it quits on this life and see what the next one offered. Despite all I had achieved, I felt that something was deeply wrong with me—that I was defective at the core. I was hollow inside, and the emptiness hurt. That day on the cliff was an awakening. It was the beginning of understanding the root of true happiness and contentment and rejecting what society had defined as success. It was the beginning of discovering—and removing—the restrictions that I had imposed on myself.

WARNING: LIMITING BELIEFS AHEAD

The things that held me back were deeply ingrained and reinforced daily by society and my industry, so much so that they were often disguised as normal attitudes and desires that most of us accept without question. That disguise made them hard to identify but, with a little thought and insight, I started to uncover the causes of the beliefs that had stopped me—and that may be stopping you—from achieving the happiness and true success we all deserve.

Here are some of the common beliefs I've found. Most of them applied to me and were holding me back. I call them "limiting beliefs" because we comply with these restrictions without challenge. As you read them, place a check mark next to each one that is holding *you* back.

- ❏ **A difficult childhood holds me back.** My childhood wasn't easy. My parents divorced when I was eleven, and I wanted to move back to California with my dad, but my whole life was in Colorado. I felt he had abandoned me. We were always financially challenged. Money was tight, the other kids knew it, and they didn't let me forget it. On top of that, I was overweight. My self-image was rock bottom, and I was picked on relentlessly by schoolmates whose circumstances weren't any better than mine. We were all in the same boat in small-town America and, without knowing it, we had accepted the limiting belief that a small, economically depressed town inflicts: *this is my benchmark standard, and it's the best that I deserve.*

- **An easy childhood holds me back.** This wasn't my problem, but it is for many of us—spending childhood in comfortable surroundings, with everything anyone could want or need. Never struggling, never having to be patient, and upon reaching adulthood, not knowing how to cope with the challenges and setbacks of everyday life. The contradiction, of course, is that an easy childhood is exactly what so many of us want to provide for our children, but we don't realize the limiting belief that comes with it in adulthood: *this is the best that I can do, and life will never be as good as it used to be.*

- **A bad relationship holds me back.** I spent years craving the love, affection, and attention that was missing from my youth. Combine this with my low self-image and society's image of a perfect marriage, and it's a recipe for disaster. I got married far too young, at nineteen years old, and my wife and I lived parallel lives, going through the motions of a marriage without the benefits of passion or camaraderie. After she left, which was for the better, I did what so many people do, and I settled. I reconnected with and married my high school sweetheart, and we had a ten-year marriage that was nothing more than dysfunction for the better part of half of our time together. We eventually separated, as we should have, but only later did I realize that I lacked a good model for a successful marriage: my parents had been married eleven times between them (seven times for Dad and four for Mom). As I thought about that (and about so many other failed marriages), I realized a common denominator: *we settle for the partner we think we deserve.*

- **My body holds me back.** Society and the media bombard us with images of the perfect body. On TV, in the movies, in advertising, in print, and in video, we face an endless onslaught of toned models and muscular figures that few of us can match. How does it affect your self-image when you look in the mirror every day and see someone who doesn't quite measure up? It's a constant undercurrent of unworthiness: *I am unattractive to myself and others.*

- **My lack of education holds me back.** Society tells us that a college education is the key to success. It's also increasingly expensive, saddling students with debt that might take decades to repay. The trades are a perfect example of how you don't need a college degree to create and live an incredibly successful life. However, many of those who lack a degree toil away in low-paying, menial jobs even when they have the mind and the ability to do far better, even without a formal education. But society tells them otherwise, so they stay put in dead-end jobs: *I didn't get the education I need, so this job is all I deserve.*

- **My level of achievement holds me back.** This is a particular problem for those of us who grew up in small towns or attended small schools. You may have been a top student, a great athlete, a popular personality, the class clown—you name it. But when you moved on to a new community, to college/vocational school, to the armed forces, or to a new job, you found out you weren't as exceptional as you thought you were. Other people were smarter, funnier, or better athletes. It's a demoralizing confidence-buster that can make you question everything you thought you knew about yourself. Some of us never recover: *I'm as good as I can ever be, and I don't want the pain of comparing myself to others who are better.*

- **My lack of qualifications holds me back.** This is a close cousin of *imposter syndrome*: the feeling that you aren't qualified for your position or role. It's a common phenomenon that brings with it the fear of being unmasked as someone who has no business doing what you're doing and that everything you've worked for will come crashing down in ruins when you're discovered. The real damage, though, is that it can stifle ambition. Back in 1994, when I left my job at the lumberyard and started my drain cleaning company, I struggled tremendously with this thought process: *I'm not good enough to be where I am, so I don't dare try for anything better.*

- **Slavery to the norms holds me back.** This is the big one, and in some ways, it's the sum total of everything else on this list. Society tells us what success should look like, what our bodies should look like, what sort of education we should have, how our marriages should be conducted, and that's just the tip of the iceberg. It is a nonstop assault by television and social media. Slavery to the norms is so pervasive that it's almost invisible, but it's present in everything we think and believe: *not honoring my true desires and attempting to live for other people's ideal of me holds me back.*

How many more can you think of that I didn't mention? Take a moment to list three of them right here:

_____

_____

_____

Limiting beliefs may hold a person back, but they can also push a person to drive forward and create a life they don't truly desire or have passion about. This shows up in many millionaires with estranged marriages, poor relationships with children, and the ever-so-famous midlife crises. When we allow limiting beliefs to operate unchecked or unchallenged, we subconsciously end up with results we didn't want, which are simply a reflection of behavior created from the beliefs we were taught and accepted.

In my case, I got to the brink of ending my life. Fortunately for me, I was able to do the work to get out of my pain and learn the recipe for success that worked for me and my own human experience. Others aren't so lucky. This is your chance to honor the true gut feeling inside of you that is asking you to do something different or better than what you've been doing currently in life, business, relationships, and finances.

THE SILVER LINING ADVANTAGE

The good news is that there is NOTHING wrong with you. Limiting beliefs are exactly that—*beliefs*. And like any belief, they can be changed. The first step is identifying them and seeing them for what they are. That's why I made a list. As you examine your life and business and isolate your own limiting beliefs, consider how the circumstances of that belief have actually improved your life—find the silver lining. Maybe a difficult childhood made you mentally stronger, or a bad relationship taught you something about *good* relationships, or a lack of formal education fostered a work ethic that allowed you to compete and succeed against those who had college degrees.

Whatever the case may be, I guarantee that there are positive aspects to wherever you are, and those positive aspects are gifts. They are secret weapons that *you* don't even know you have. The challenges that you've spent a lifetime living with and struggling to overcome are your unique advantages, lessons that only you have learned, lessons that can propel you forward, but only if you find them and use them. They're the stairway to the next level of your life and career. Identify them and harness them. They are the keys to your future.

I want to share a few examples with you of people who were not only able to break free from their limiting beliefs but who found their silver lining advantage in the challenges they faced. Each turned their life into something positive, accomplishing things they would never have without the challenges life threw at them.

My late friend Sean Stephenson was born with osteogenesis imperfecta. Commonly known as brittle bone disease, it is a disorder that left him at three feet tall, and if he sneezed, he would fracture ribs. He had one of the most challenging physical lives I've ever personally witnessed and could have easily become a victim of his life circumstances. But, because he didn't accept a belief that he was "less than" or there was something wrong with him, he became one of the most inspiring motivational speakers ever, authoring great books and creating life-changing coaching, training, and positive impact on people's lives, including my own.

A friend and client of mine, who we'll call Joe for anonymity purposes, spent many years in federal prison for a form of white-collar crimes. After he was released from prison and got his life on track, he became a contractor and now owns and operates one of the most successful contracting businesses in the United States. If he had accepted the belief that he was a bad person because of his previous actions, he definitely would have recreated his past and almost certainly be back in prison.

Another lifelong friend of mine got caught up in the real estate boom back in the early 2000s. As a contractor, he ended up getting into some poor investments that he couldn't get out of and faced filing bankruptcy. That action was against everything he ever stood for or believed. He would say, "Bad people file bankruptcy, reckless people file bankruptcy . . . losers file bankruptcy." After doing a lot of work together exposing his own beliefs of his self-worth and honoring that his circumstances were different from running up credit cards or spending money he didn't have, he decided to file bankruptcy and become a schoolteacher. He has enjoyed an incredibly rewarding career teaching construction for the local school district career center. He has become financially independent (on a teacher's salary), and he will be retiring in a few short years at the young age of fifty-five.

THE SECRET OF SUCCESS

Well, it's *one* of the secrets: it's the ability to see things differently. One element that separates truly successful people from the general population is an optimistic point of view. Where most of us see setbacks, successful people see opportunities. Where most of us see painful difficulties, successful people see constructive challenges. Every limiting belief can be reframed as a challenge that, instead of holding you back, makes you better and stronger.

Do you feel unqualified for your current job? Accept the reality of your position; work to solidify your performance and build the trust of those around you. There is a broken belief around "fake it till you make it," and we think if we are learning something while doing it, then we are poseurs. The reality is that EVERYONE was once unqualified for the job that they are now masters at. When I started out in a truck by myself, I had no business being in business, but by diligence, accepting the learning curve, and never giving up, I was able to eventually become the market leader in my craft.

Got burned in a bad relationship? Remember what you learned and strive to make the next one better. When we're going through it, we sometimes forget that we have some responsibility as well. Regardless of the situation, we must take full ownership not just of our own actions, but more importantly, the lessons learned from the "getting burned" experience. I know I would not have the great marriage *The Lovely Christy* and I enjoy had we both not been through (and learned from) very challenging relationships in the past.

Feeling like you aren't as good as you thought you were? Understand that most of the people you're comparing yourself to feel the same way and that you'll never be better than you believe yourself to be. A comparison mindset is one of the most damaging thinking activities possible. When we compare ourselves to others—or what we "should" be—we are often left feeling deflated or disappointed. Only when we adopt a mindset and core belief that we are always doing our best will our reality make a major shift regarding personal fulfillment.

I had a hard time adopting the belief that everyone is doing the best they can. I would challenge Marcus, my personal coach at the time, with things like, "Wait a minute, I'm supposed to believe that when I was selling drugs in Lake Havasu City, Arizona, back in the late eighties, I was doing the best I could? I don't buy it!" He was very patient as I would slowly come down from my rant, and he helped me find my own truth that I ended up adopting, which is, yes, I was doing the best I could at that very moment in time with the place I was in my life. Based on parents, peers, previous conditioning, and the unconscious programming I was operating from, I was doing the very best I could. Otherwise, I would have done better! This is true for everyone around us at all times.

Every time you find yourself stymied by a limiting belief, the feeling that some aspect of your life holds you back, remember that the way you *think* about that obstacle is entirely under your control, even when the circumstances aren't. I know people who lost their jobs only to realize later that losing a job was *the best thing that ever happened to them*. It opened their minds to opportunities and ideas that would otherwise have been closed to them, and they went on to become far more successful than they ever were before. They didn't allow a job loss to become a limiting belief. Instead, they let it be a stepping-stone to greatness. It isn't easy to look at something as difficult as a job loss and see an opportunity. I get it. But you can do it. And if you can do that, you can do it with just about any obstacle or setback that stands in your way.

Sometimes what seems impossible isn't, and what appears to be the end of the world is just the start of something better.

Little did I know, when I looked over the edge of that cliff at the Colorado National Monument, that it was the beginning of seeing my life in a whole new way and, for the first time ever, becoming truly alive.

Look back at the limiting beliefs you checked off and listed earlier. Grab a piece of paper or a notebook and start listing the positive skills and behaviors you can take away from each of them. Include how they can help you be a better and more successful leader.

CHAPTER 2

WHEN THE RIGHT PATH IS THE WRONG ROAD

I ATTENDED A FUNERAL a few years ago that followed the same pattern most funerals do: a steady stream of family and friends took the podium to tell their stories and generally say nice things about the deceased, especially about how *successful* he had been—a man who was a well-known business owner and a pillar of the community. I had known him well enough, both personally and through others, to make some sense of what the mourners were saying about him, and the longer I listened, the more troubled I became.

He had, indeed, been very successful by every conventional measure. He had a booming company, a big house, a seven-figure bank account, seats on multiple boards, and he was the target of those who sought influence and advice. In other words, he appeared to be exactly the sort of person that so many of us strive to be.

He had followed the path to what is considered "success." But his success came with a cost. He was a functioning alcoholic, dangerously overweight, with a string of divorces behind him, offspring who took no interest in him unless they needed something, and a life span cut short far too early by bad habits and, maybe, by a bad state of mind. Naturally, no one pointed these things out at his funeral. That's not how funerals work. But they were true, and the disconnect between the reality and the perception was startling. The more I thought about it, the more it bothered me. Right this very moment, millions of people are seeking the kind of success—the success that comes at the expense of family, health, and relationships—that helped push this gentleman into an early grave. The worst thing is, most of them will never know the damage it does until it's too late. I've seen this happen too often in the trades, and it has motivated me to help home service leaders stop heading down this path of insanity.

THE MYTH OF SACRIFICE

Even when we're aware of this damage, we often find ourselves excusing it as the price we must pay to achieve success. I knew a contractor who stayed in a different town five days a week and only saw his family, including two young children, on the weekends. It was the sacrifice he was willing to make for the big house, the expensive car, the four-wheel-drive toys, and all the other trappings of success. It was easy to envy him until you peeked beneath the surface. He had virtually abandoned his family in exchange for the appearance of great wealth and being a successful contractor. Living the dream, right?

We've developed a culture where we're almost made to feel guilty if we don't sacrifice for success; this is painfully evident in the home service industry. How many times have you heard someone proudly say that they haven't taken a vacation in years? How often do people avoid taking a sick day because they feel like they'd be blacklisted for doing so? I used to feel this way. In fact, I created a fear-based culture in one of my service businesses that encouraged these feelings and behaviors, one where everything was predicated upon loyalty and devotion to the business. I demanded that team members live and breathe the company, so much so that the general manager had our logo tattooed on his arm (that was his own choice, of course . . . or was there more to it?). I'm not proud of this today, but it's part of what made me realize that I was heading down the wrong road. And I learned one of the reasons why this lifestyle is so hard to quit.

Being the sacrificing professional, the hard worker, and the devoted leader (putting in the most time and effort) becomes integral to our identity. It becomes who we are, and who are we if we aren't that? I certainly don't disparage hard work or devotion to a good company or cause—on the contrary, both of these can be good and healthy aspects of our identity—but when these things become central to our very being, it's time to take a step back and reconsider what we're doing and get back to who we are at our core. The challenge is that reevaluating something so central to our identity can make us feel lost and adrift—as if we no longer know who we are or where we fit in the world. But we *do* know who we are. We just might have to rediscover it.

The issues of sacrifice and identity can build to a third issue that is even more insidious than the other two: putting off what you really want to do for a hypothetical tomorrow that may never arrive. My stepdad worked five and a half days a week, nonstop, never took a break, hardly took a vacation. While he was a good provider, he and my mom were completely held hostage by his career, always in a holding pattern, always waiting for a time when he would retire and they could travel and take vacations and enjoy all of the good things that had been sacrificed in the name of success. In the meantime, his children had moved away, Mom was eagerly awaiting his retirement, and then sadly, he became ill with early-onset dementia at just sixty years old, only to die a few short years later. The promise of tomorrow was never realized, and it's hard to enjoy the fruits of success from the grave.

I know people who wait for everything to be perfect before they start taking action on what they truly want to do with their lives. The reality is that there is no perfect time to start living life on your terms; actually, there is ONLY one perfect time for this, and that time is now. It always has been now, and it always will be now. Truly all we have is the present moment. Don't dismiss this as being cliché; this is a vastly important realization to embrace. Most people spend every present moment of their lives fantasizing about the future, which may or may not come, or they fixate on living in the reflection of the past, which can only be recalled in the present moment. The only time you can actually do anything is right now. Yes, you take steps to organize and plan for the future but be cautious of your beliefs and subconscious mind, which are always justifying why you should wait to take action on the life and business of your dreams.

You've probably heard this one: the definition of insanity is doing the same thing over and over and expecting a different result. That's a good definition, but I have another one: the definition of insanity is working yourself into an early grave, alienating your family, and sacrificing your own happiness and health because that's what society expects you to do. It's true! Our culture glorifies the model of nonstop nose-to-the-grindstone labor and makes us feel guilty if we don't fit that model. It's a success trap: we get on the treadmill and find it impossible to escape. We become cogs in a perpetual-motion machine, unable to free ourselves, and in doing so, our pursuit of happiness makes us miserable. Ironic, isn't it?

ROADBLOCKS

While it is crucial to take stock in the path we are on, we must also be aware of what mental roadblocks may surface. The more you take action on your dreams, the more activity you create. The more activity you create, the more potential roadblocks can arise, which will need to be handled one at a time. Some of the most damaging are the mental roadblocks we allow to come forward from our past experiences or what we've been taught by society—in other words, limiting beliefs.

I want to address a few more limiting beliefs, specifically regarding success, that we need to put in the rearview mirror. Again, check off each one that applies to you.

- ❑ **A college education is essential.** No, it isn't. And the belief that it is can destroy lives. College educations become harder to attain every year, and every generation carries a heavier debt load of college loans than the one that came before. I'm not putting down education. Far from it! I'm in the education business, and I hope you learn all you can. But society continues to insist that we can't succeed without a degree, and if we don't have one, we might never aim higher than waiting tables or punching cash registers. Society tells us that, without college, that's all we're good for. Nonsense. I never finished college. Neither did most of my successful clients, including the wealthiest people I know (and I know some pretty wealthy people). You can be fabulously successful without a degree. We must believe this and share this knowledge to empower our entire industry and add young, hungry, and talented people to our ranks.

- ❑ **You'll never get ahead working a blue-collar job.** I did. My clients did. You probably did. And there are plenty of others who have built great lives for themselves and their families through blue-collar work. But again, society tells us that a blue-collar job is a one-way ticket to drudgery and near-poverty. If you're willing to go along with that, then drudgery and near-poverty may be in your future. This is the problematic mindset that many young people have been fed, including most prospects you currently interview. Our job as leaders is to help them think beyond what society expects and uncover a very different reality for themselves and our entire industry.

- **I can do it all by myself!** No, you can't, and neither can anyone else. Too many people labor under the idea that collaboration is weakness. We're conditioned to value individual achievement over group accomplishment. The truth is that collaboration often saves time, saves money, and saves your sanity—all of which are keys to a new kind of success that doesn't align with the trails that society has blazed for us.

- **Do what you love, and the money will follow.** Or the alternate version: love what you do, and you'll never work another day in your life. Sadly, this isn't often true. I love to watch movies, but I've never earned a dime from it, and I don't expect that to change. I also don't expect most of the current generation to earn a living playing video games (yes, I know there are exceptions, but they're few and far between). Loving what you do is an ideal. Maybe you'll get lucky, but don't get hung up on it. Loving what you do at a deeper level than the task itself (connection to your purpose) is what is essential to building the life of your dreams.

Are there other ways you've allowed society's definitions of success to control your own life and career? List a few.

_____

_____

_____

THE ROAD LESS TRAVELED

It's time to rethink our pathways to success and, moreover, to rethink what success actually is. The current models are restrictive and, sometimes, destructive (as we have seen). We live under the assumption that we can't have it all, that work-life balance is a myth, that we have to sacrifice sanity and happiness at the altar of work—in other words, that we can't have our cake and eat it too. I'm telling you that you can. I do it every day and so do many of my clients.

The key is to change how we think about success. What really makes you happy? Is it working twelve-hour days? Probably not, though some of my clients love what they do so much they work long hours by choice. How about money in the bank? That's definitely necessary, but at the core, it's not what ultimately makes you happy. Stop for a moment and ask yourself (maybe even take out that notebook or paper again): What does success really mean to you? What truly makes you happy? How about time with your family, being home at a reasonable time, enjoying the weekends, cultivating your talents, taking vacations while your children—and you—are still young, and having a mind free of undue stress and worry. You can have all of that *and* earn a great living as a successful leader. It's all a matter of redefining your goals—your purpose—and taking the path that can get you where you want to be in a way that might defy society's expectations.

I was intrigued when I met Keith Cunningham a few years ago at a mastermind event. Keith is the author of *The Road Less Stupid* and a speaker at Tony Robbins's Wealth Mastery and Business Mastery events. That all sounds great, but in my opinion, the greatest part of Keith's story is from February 1989 when he realized he had lost it all (and then some). Being one of the only people he knows who has lost a hundred million dollars, Keith jokes about how his education is one of the most expensive ever. But he did learn his lessons and eventually bounced back to become an incredibly successful businessperson again due to that hundred-million-dollar education. He would not be the businessperson, educator, mentor, and friend that he is if he hadn't played full out. This is true for you as well. No matter your situation, you can learn the lessons necessary to adapt and overcome any challenges.

My buddy Joe Polish was a struggling carpet cleaner who had dealt with addiction issues most of his life. He ended up buying a marketing course on a credit card because he needed to find a way to clean enough carpets to eat, and from that moment in time, the rest, as they say, is history. Joe now runs Genius Network, a high-level entrepreneur mastermind group, and has personally become one of the leading authorities in the world on direct marketing.

My friend Jim Dew, the co-founder of Dew Wealth, a firm that Christy and I utilize to help manage our own investments and finances, came from a challenging background. His parents grew up in the great depression, and he constantly heard stories about money and hardship. He now knows that was good in a way because it made him respect the security of money. But he also shares he began feeling that being poor was honorable. He actually found himself trying to act like he was poor to make his dad proud. His mom was a huge help in changing his mindset and direction by lecturing him with, "You act like it's a great thing to be poor. Your father and I were poor, and it's not a great thing to be poor. And by the way, you're not poor. You're not in a poor family." This helped Jim realize that the reality of the stories he heard about his parents and grandparents while growing up did not have to become his own reality. Because he changed this belief, he and his awesome wife, Mimi, have been able to build an incredibly successful life together, as well as helping others do the same.

True success—success that brings happiness for yourself and your loved ones, without the side effects of ill health, endless stress, and absence from your family—can be yours when you lead a life of *purpose* instead of shackling yourself to society's definition of success.

CHAPTER 3

PURPOSELY PUTTING THE INSANITY BEHIND YOU

"YOU DON'T UNDERSTAND," I said. "I own a 24/7 service company with forty-two team members. It's an endless litany of early mornings, late nights, urgent phone calls, demanding texts, emergencies, dumpster fires, crises, personnel issues, team squabbling, deadlines, and sleeplessness. How can you tell me to 'Be more Zen'? I don't have time to be Zen. I barely have time to eat! Am I supposed to just take off and sit on a mountain top in a lotus position? I can't!"

I'd had some doubts about my mentor before, but this took the cake. Couldn't he see what was going on around me, the whirlwind that threatened to engulf everything the moment I turned my back? It's easy to say that I should step back and relax, but I felt like that was out of touch with reality. I couldn't afford to step away, to disengage, to trust the fate of my company to the cosmos.

And yet . . . a few years later, I spent six months traveling the country in a motor home while my company chugged along growing profitably without me. How did I do that?

It took some work. It took some adjustment. And it took a massive change of thought and philosophy. It took purpose-guided leadership.

PURPOSE-GUIDED LEADERSHIP

The situation that I described above—of being so wrapped up in the day-to-day details of life that you can never have a moment's peace—happens all too often to far too many people. It's a natural occurrence that stems from two common issues: *focusing on limiting beliefs* and *focusing on our immediate goals and needs*.

When we focus on limiting beliefs, we fixate upon what we've convinced ourselves we can't do, which can make us prisoners of our routine. We've already spent some quality time discussing limiting beliefs, and we'll discuss more in later chapters. Until you can move past those, putting aside the boundaries that you've grown to accept without question, you can never embrace all that you're capable of being.

Moving on to the second issue. By focusing on our immediate goals and needs, we fixate on what it takes just to get through the day, and we set ourselves up to repeat that day *forever*. The key to this issue, and the secret that can allow you to spend six months in an RV, is purpose-guided living. Obviously, even when you're waist-deep in daily problems, you are still living your life with a sense of purpose. It's just that your purpose might be limited to making sure that your business is still running in sixty minutes' time, or seeing to it that your kids get off to school before the bus leaves, or ensuring that there's something to eat for supper. These kinds of extremely short-term goals are necessary and important, but it's too easy to let them eclipse the longer-term goals that, when achieved, make it possible for us to live the life of our dreams. And believe me, with the right focus, you can achieve so much more than just the chores and tasks of daily existence. In other words, instead of focusing on what gets you through the next hour, focus on what will allow you to spend six months in an RV (or whatever your passion might be). Easier said than done, right?

I once had a long conversation with someone who grew up on the American home front during World War II. We discussed rationing, scrap drives, victory gardens, shared sacrifice, and the missing young men who had been sent overseas to fight. While all of this was fascinating, there was one thing that he said that really struck me and that has stayed with me ever since: "In those days, you always asked yourself the same question, all day every day: *how is what I am doing right now helping to win the war?*"

You are fighting a war right now—a war for your life—and everything you do influences its outcome, but before you can judge the value of your actions, you have to establish your goals. During World War II, the purpose was clear: defeat the Axis powers and preserve Western democracy. How did we do that? We built a military force that could cross oceans and take the fight to the enemy. And how did we do *that*? The people became engaged in the purpose: men joined the service, women moved to the factories, companies switched to military production, senior citizens staffed civil defense boards, children collected scrap, and everyone bought war bonds and conserved resources.

If we had stayed focused on our day-to-day lives, as many were before the bombing of Pearl Harbor, the war effort would have gone nowhere. It was only when we expanded the scope of our vision and took on a larger challenge that things started to happen. Now let's scale things down a little: I was in a hectic situation, running a company that consumed my every waking moment and going nowhere exactly because my every waking moment was consumed by running the company. The prospect of spending six months in an RV sounded like heaven. (Can you relate?) As impossible as it seemed, I decided to go for it. *Now I had a purpose that was bigger than simple day-to-day survival.* But how could I get there? I would have to rebuild my company in a way that would allow it to operate without me. That meant training my people to be leaders and managers, empowering them to take greater responsibility, and then—crucially—stepping back and allowing them to do it.

That last part is a doozy. For many of us, it's the hardest part of all. As unpleasant as being shackled to stress and crises can be, it also makes us feel needed and necessary. If we can uncouple from our company, then what's the point of us being there at all? The point is this: the company is there to enable you to live the life that you choose to live. If you're a leader who doesn't own the business, the point is the same: your job should enable you to live the life that you choose. If it doesn't, then you have a new short-term purpose: have a conversation for clarity with the owner or find a different job.

If this sounds awfully selfish, think again. In building a company that enabled me to take a six-month road trip, I also built a company that worked far better for my team than the old one did. Empowering my people to become leaders and managers meant developing them, teaching them new skills and new ways of looking at things. They, too, had to expand their vision beyond their day-to-day tasks to see the larger picture and understand their roles in it. It simply made them *better people*. It did the same for me.

Take special notice of one thing I said above: the company worked far better for my team than the old one did. *The company worked for the people.* And it gave all of us something that we hadn't had before—it made us look at our lives through the lens of purpose.

Once you have a purpose, it's time to revisit that question from the World War II home front: *how is what I am doing right now helping to win the war?*

Get that notebook or paper out again. How is your purpose being executed through your daily leadership activities?

As you go through your day—and not just your workday—always be asking yourself, *How does what I am doing right now help me honor and live my purpose?* If you can honestly say that your activities are helping you build the life you want to live, then good job, you're on your way. If not, it's time to reorient your activities so that they do. More on this later, but it's not too early to start thinking about it and laying the groundwork for what's to come.

For now, the most important question to ask yourself is this: What matters most to you? More time with your family? Enough money to be secure and comfortable? The capacity to pursue hobbies and other interests? Furthering your education? A six-month trip in an RV? True emotional freedom, or at least emotional regulation? Any of these things and more are within your grasp when you live a purpose-guided life. Never let anyone tell you that you can't have it all, that you can't have both wealth and free time, that it's impossible to balance your work and personal lives. Every day my clients prove it's all possible. I'm also living proof that you can. I have plenty of money, I'm still earning it, and I have the time and freedom to do most of the things I'd like to do.

So much of what we've been told is wrong. You can live a life that makes you authentically happy, that allows your family to thrive, that supports everyone around you, and that will inspire others to do the same. It means living *in* purpose and *on* purpose to *achieve* a purpose. It means gaining clarity, reorienting yourself, and making things happen. Easier said than done, right? Wrong. I'm here to tell you how.

EFFECTIVE LEADERSHIP

Think about someone who has demonstrated effective leadership in your own life. They could be from many years ago or someone who you're enjoying in your life right now. A teacher, a pastor, a sports coach—get a clear memory of them and hold them in your mind. What are the attributes they utilized that made such a positive influence in your life? Trust? Integrity? Holding you accountable? Firm but fair? Whatever things helped you are also some of the same things you can use to help others. We know how hard it seems to be to find good leaders. Why? Because it's not always easy to maintain the necessary behaviors of quality leadership. Social pressures, budgets, expectations, and egos all come into play when it comes to leaders "doing the right thing."

Now more than ever, your team needs you to show up as the best possible leader you can be. To do that, you need to be clear about your biggest strengths and take off the blinders regarding what you need to do to improve clarity, communication, and execution of your role in the business. It's often said that effective leadership is simply executing the company's vision. BORING! There is a lot more complexity to leadership than that definition.

Your team is begging for a vision to be shared, yes. But in addition to that vision, they also need and desire you to lead by example. By the way, all that means is doing the best you can. Nobody is asking you to be perfect. Don't avoid hard truths; take responsibility for your own actions as well as those of the team. Show up with and convey an optimistic and growth mindset while creating a safe environment to express their creativity in reaching company goals.

When leaders operate intending to keep ego at bay and always do their best from a place of trust, love, and vulnerability, entire organizations thrive. I've personally operated both with an iron fist, hiding behind my ego and addictions, as well as learning to come from a place of love, empathy, and true vulnerability. This led me to understand how the Blue Collar Success Laws I'm about to share will change your life and organization forever when adopted and applied effectively. Let's jump into the first law and open your mind right now.

CHAPTER 4

LAW #1 AUTHENTIC ABUNDANCE

EVERYDAY LIFE CAN BE A GRIND. We're so focused on simple survival that we never pause to consider that all of life's abundance, everything that it has to offer, is within our grasp. Too many of us are held in thrall by *scarcity thinking*, the belief that there will never be enough—never enough money, never enough time, never enough of anything that can make us feel comfortable and secure. It's a perfectly natural state of mind; after all, we *do* need money to pay for food, clothing, and shelter, but settling for a survival mindset condemns us to spend our days burdened by stress, worry, and joyless toil, never achieving true abundance.

I was in that very place, sweating my day-to-day existence, when I was introduced to someone who had built a phenomenally successful HVAC company, exactly the sort of enterprise that, at the time, I assumed was beyond my abilities to create. Amazingly, before I had done more than say hello, he asked me about *my* company. I told him it was nothing much, that we were getting by, but it was hard to earn enough money to make payroll and still have what I needed to keep food on my own table.

He said, "And as long as you keep thinking that way, your company will never be better than *nothing much*. You have to expand your vision and see everything that you, and your company, can become and stop assuming that where you are now is as far as you can go."

At first, I objected. I *did* want to be successful. Doesn't everyone? But the more I thought about it, the more I realized that he was correct. He had seen right through me and my limited mindset. Even though I wanted to be successful, I was focused on my limitations. My company was struggling for survival, and I was obsessed with continuing the struggle instead of rising above it.

I was fighting for survival instead of embracing abundance, sacrificing my long-term goals and success on the altar of my daily needs, and depriving myself of the authentic abundance that I—and you—deserve. I was very fortunate, though, in one way: *someone pointed out that I was in a rut and told me to get out of it*. Some of us never achieve that realization.

WHAT IS AUTHENTIC ABUNDANCE?

When most of us think of abundance, we think of *things*—cars, jewelry, a big house, expensive electronics—and *money*. Lots of *things* and lots of *money*: exactly what society has conditioned us to think that we need. But if abundance also means *plenty*, can we find it by accumulating possessions and filling our bank accounts when the net result of those activities is always an insatiable desire for more?

The answer is no; we can't. True, authentic abundance isn't found in the material world. It isn't measured by your bottom line or by an expensive home filled with fancy, expensive luxuries. Let's be crystal clear, I *love* nice things and am in no way saying you shouldn't have expensive things or everything you desire when it comes to material possessions. I'm just reminding you of what you already know: there's more to it than what meets the eye. Authentic abundance is about fulfillment and being centered in true happiness—*your* true happiness. And here's the best part: authentic abundance is something that you share with those around you.

This is a real stretch for many of us, and I understand the challenge it can pose. It was a challenge for me, too, and it took some help to make me understand it. In my case, a few friends had convinced me to start taking yoga classes. *Sure*, I thought, *why not?* It couldn't hurt, and it would probably help with my overall fitness goals. (I'm always open to trying something new that has seemed to work well for others.) However, I didn't realize that yoga is as much a *psychological* exercise as a physical one—maybe even more so. I learned to really slow down, to allow my mind and my thoughts to go from my usual mile-a-minute pace to a relaxed, one-thought-at-a-time drip. It was like going from a hundred-yard dash to a leisurely country stroll.

The hundred-yard dash has its uses, but it's the country stroll that lets you come to terms with who you are and how you've been using your time and your talents—that lets you consider the world that you've built for yourself and how your friends, family, and coworkers fit into it.

Yoga gave me a glimpse into the peace and serenity I needed to get in touch with my own concept of authentic abundance, free from the pressures and influences of the outside world and my perception of success in the trades. What gives you peace and serenity? How can you clear your mind and tame your thoughts? Maybe it's yoga, or maybe it's meditation, deep prayer, or even a few minutes on the couch with your favorite beverage. Find what works for you and learn to slow down. However, I do not recommend using any forms of drugs or alcohol in the pursuit of peace, happiness, or calming the mind. I tried every combination of mind-altering substances for many years, and things didn't turn around for me until I became sober for life. The ability to consciously slow the mind and create self-reflective thinking time is foundational for everything else that follows in this book.

You may be wondering how *authentic* plays into this new view of abundance. The word authentic gets thrown around a lot. The trinkets they sell on TV always include certificates of authenticity, somehow guaranteeing that whatever it is they're hawking is the real deal. In the context of authentic abundance, *authentic* doesn't just mean that it's real and true; it means that it's true to *you*—the author of your life—and uniquely yours. Your authentic abundance isn't mine, and mine isn't someone else's. It's something that is yours, and yours alone, and you have to discover it for yourself. But remember, authentic abundance isn't a goal; it's a way of thinking and a way of life—a way that lets you live in contentment and peace even if you don't possess the material wealth that so many others use to measure their success. Authentic abundance grants you a calm and stability that don't rely upon outside influences for affirmation. It allows you to weather the storms that blow away people who lack inner reserves of strength.

You may ask, how do I achieve my own authentic abundance?

Step 1: Eliminate scarcity thinking. Scarcity thinking is the belief that there are limits on who you are and what you're capable of becoming. Scarcity thinking is resigning yourself to your current situation, surrendering to the curse of mediocrity. If you think you can't significantly improve your world—your *personal* world—or that you can't go beyond the precedents that your family has already set, then you are a victim of scarcity thinking. The first step in eliminating this scourge is awareness. You can't purge scarcity thinking from your mind if you don't know it's there. When you slow down your mind and let your thoughts stretch out, ask yourself how you might be holding yourself back with scarcity thinking. What you discover might surprise you. With this awareness, you can make a conscious choice to always make your future bigger than your past. For assistance in eliminating your scarcity thinking right now, make sure to utilize my abundance thinking tool at *www.BlueCollarBook.com*.

❏ **Scarcity thinking.** Let's be honest. Scarcity thinking is a limiting belief of authentic abundance (and there are more), so check it off if it applies.

Step 2: Embrace your personal purpose. What is your purpose? What sort of life do you want to live? What sort of person do you want to be? It's okay to be specific here. Remember my RV trip in Chapter 1? You can envision that for yourself—maybe it's setting up your office under a palm tree on a beach in the Bahamas or simply living a life free from undue stress and anxiety. Those are all reasonable and achievable. Or maybe it's something bigger, like living a life that allows you to make a positive difference in the lives of others. Whatever it is for you, trust your gut and honor your own truth. And that brings us to Step 3:

Step 3: Embrace your company/family purpose. Now expand your personal purpose to your family. Make them a part of what you plan for yourself. How do you envision your family's future? How can your influence improve their lives? How can it strengthen your bonds and help resolve the disputes and squabbles that plague every family from time to time?

Are you in a position of leadership and/or influence at your workplace? (Hint: If you have a job at all, you are in a position of influence in your workplace.) Expand your purpose to include your fellow team members and your employer. How can your workplace be better? How can you help make it that way? What kind of company do you want to work for, and how can you shape its future? If you're the owner or a high-level manager, you'll have a lot of levers of power to make this happen, but even an entry-level team member who just started an hour ago has some influence and can help make a positive change in the people around them. Don't take this step too lightly; your fulfillment at work and with family is paramount to life mastery.

Step 4: Blend your personal and company/family purposes. Ultimately, your personal purpose and your company/family purpose are one and the same. Your personal purpose can't constantly be at odds with your life as part of a group. Bring them into alignment and, together, they will transform you. There is truly no such thing as personal life, family life, and business life anyway. There is simply a life; it's yours, and you get the opportunity to fill it with a mix of family, business, and other activities that YOU desire.

WHAT STANDS IN MY WAY?

Those limiting beliefs—they are never far away:

- ❏ **I need more.** Outside influences chip away at us relentlessly. We are bombarded by messages from morning till night, from the subliminal to the obvious, telling us that we need *more*, and saying we're not good enough unless we have it. Consumer society collaborates with scarcity thinking to convince us of the necessity of accumulation: more stuff, the latest fashions, the newest models, and things we never wanted or needed until someone convinced us otherwise. Worse, our whole culture has been built around this mindset. We line up around the block to replace the phone we bought twelve months ago; we crash websites buying the video game that's sweeping the nation. It becomes part of our identity, part of our *perceived purpose*, and it all comes at us from the outside. This endless desire for more doesn't come from within; it has to be *planted* there, like an invasive vine that chokes all the good plants into submission. It's time to start up the weed whacker.

How do we uproot it? When you calm your thoughts and quiet your mind, using whatever method you choose to achieve that state, identify those outside pressures and push them firmly to the side. Recognize them for what they are: quick hits of happiness and satisfaction that ultimately leave you feeling empty and, worse, distract you from the path to your own authentic abundance.

- **I don't deserve more than what I have.** Many of us stay where we are, never reaching far beyond our current situation because we have an unspoken fear of exceeding our self-imposed limitations. This fear can manifest itself in many ways, from guilt over outperforming parents and friends to a refusal to emerge from our comfort zones and even keeping our gifts and talents hidden away from the world. This belief, this negation of self-worth, is a disease that can affect every area of your mind.

Clean it out. Tell yourself that it's okay to want what you want. It's okay to be the most successful person in your family. It's okay to want to truly have it all. It's okay to want what you want simply because you want it.

I remember years ago how hard it was for me to leave a best practices group as a very connected member and the top trainer. I knew I would be judged. I knew I would be chastised. I knew it would make others extremely uncomfortable. But I also knew I had more. I had a vision of what coaching and training could be in the trades, and I had to take the necessary actions to step into my next level of greatness. From this commitment to my own authentic abundance, the Blue Collar Success Group was born.

Marianne Williamson said it better than I can:

> Our deepest fear is not that we are inadequate. Our deepest fear is that we are powerful beyond measure. It is our light, not our darkness, that most frightens us. We ask ourselves, "Who am I to be brilliant, gorgeous, talented, fabulous?" Actually, who are you not to be? You are a child of God. Your playing small does not serve the world. There is nothing enlightened about shrinking so that other people won't feel insecure around you. We are all meant to shine, as children do. We were born to make manifest the glory of God that is within us. It's not just in some of us; it's in everyone. And as we let our own light shine, we unconsciously give other people permission to

do the same. As we are liberated from our own fear, our presence automatically liberates others.

Discovering your authentic abundance is discovering your authentic self. When you strip away the things that pollute your mind, that obscure your thinking, and distract you from your true purpose, you'll find out who you really are and who you're meant to become. Seize the opportunity and make the discovery.

CHAPTER 5

LAW #2 RELATIONSHIPS BEFORE RESULTS

WHAT IF I TOLD YOU that there is a way to never worry about being judged by other people, a way you could believe in and practice the religion you want, worship in a way that makes the most sense to you, and have a bank account that grows every month, all while experiencing the greatest confidence and self-esteem you've ever had. Would you call me crazy? Read on.

This is a good place to point out that all of the things we've talked about up to this point are building to something, and this is the next step. Banishment of your limiting beliefs, awareness of your own authentic abundance, and an ability to calm your thoughts and get in touch with your innermost self are essential components that you need to work on as we forge ahead. Notice I didn't say that you have to *master* them. You may never master them, and that's okay. The important thing is that you're aware of these things, they're on your mind, and you're actively working on them, making them parts of your being.

Up to now, we've focused on what's going on within ourselves. It's been an inward-focused journey. With our attention on *Relationships before Results*, we'll begin to think about how we relate to ourselves and how what's going on inside us relates to—and is influenced by—outside influences like money, spirituality, and other people. We are surrounded by these forces every day, and a purpose-guided life requires knowledge of what they are and how we handle them.

Bear in mind that most people give scant thought to these things. They coast through life sleeping, eating, working, shopping, and watching TV, all of it on an endless loop. Awareness and a desire to change, to be something more, are at the heart of what separates the purpose-guided from the purposeless.

Many relationships have limiting beliefs present, and they are often interwoven between the relationships we are about to discuss. How you have been navigating and participating in the relationships below is simply based on the conditioning you've had to this point in your life. Remember, you are a byproduct of your choices, not your circumstances, but sometimes we "choose" circumstances based on subconscious programming, which dates all the way back to our childhood. Be easy with yourself as you read the next section and see where you can identify any limiting beliefs or beliefs that others may hold strongly but no longer have to be present in your own belief system. Make sure you look for specific times, circumstances, people, and events in your life as you explore the four critical relationships.

CRITICAL RELATIONSHIP #1: YOUR RELATIONSHIP WITH MONEY

What's your money mindset? Do you save as much as you can? Do you spend it as fast as you get it? Do you plan for the future or live in the moment? Like many things, the money mindset is a spectrum, and we're all on it somewhere.

The world is awash in advice about money and what to do with it. Some say the key to wealth is buying and selling real estate. That's great if you want to spend all of your time scouting properties and brokering deals. Others say to never use credit cards. This may work for some, but sometimes there's an emergency, or you need to make a high-ticket purchase and a credit card is the best way to handle it. I once subscribed to the idea that the best way to become financially secure was to be excessively frugal: you can be a millionaire if you're willing to drive a thirty-year-old car and eat Hamburger Helper every night. If that's the way you have to live, then what's the point of being a millionaire?

This mindset damaged me. I was focused on money itself instead of what money can do. Money is a *tool*. It's a means to an end, not an end in itself. It was a long time before I came around to this way of thinking.

And how did I wind up on the wrong path? I inherited my attitudes about money from my parents: *Be frugal. Get a good job. Work hard. Seek promotions. Save money.* None of these are wrong in and of themselves, and each has a time and a place, but when these ideas constitute the entirety of your attitudes about money, then you'll find yourself in a rut. For me, the revolution occurred when I began to focus on *what I wanted to do* and *how I could get the money I needed to do those things*. When you turn your thinking around this way, you'll find that your relationship with money becomes more intentional, more purpose-guided: *Here's what I want to do. How can I produce the funds I need to make that a reality?* This way of thinking can open the door to a world of creative ideas that might otherwise elude you. We're taught we want financial independence. What we really want is emotional independence, and part of that comes from financial stability, but that's only part of it. I know plenty of millionaires who have massive emotional baggage and fear around losing their money and the *identity* it represents.

There are some other destructive ideas that should be purged from our financial thinking. Have you ever heard that money can't buy happiness? I'm here to tell you that, in many cases, it can. The worst thing about this proverb, though, is that it implies that there's something good about *not* having money. It's an excuse. And if you still hold that money can't buy happiness, then at least spend some time pondering the concept of dead-broke happiness. Money can't buy happiness, but dead-broke can buy squat! As for me, I'll take the money *and* the happiness.

The other is the idea that someone with an expensive car, watch, house, you name it, must be *compensating for something*. Maybe, but it's more likely that he just likes Lamborghinis and had the funds to buy one. Again, like *Money can't buy happiness*, this is used as a defense mechanism by those who lack money and don't want to change the way that they think about it. This isn't always the case, and I'm not pretending that ego doesn't influence purchases, but if you want a Lambo and you have the dough, then don't let broken thinking stop you from buying what you want.

Change your negatively conditioned mindset about money, and your relationship with money will change for the better. This will help set you free for more wealth and happiness than you ever imagined.

CRITICAL RELATIONSHIP #2: YOUR RELATIONSHIP WITH *SPIRITUALITY*

I grew up in a household where faith was ironclad and never questioned. We were expected to toe the line, and we did. I inherited this faith as an adult, and it held me back in many ways. It didn't work for me. It wasn't fulfilling. I have a strong curiosity gene, and I'm not a cat! (Were you ever told curiosity killed the cat?) I set out to study the five major religions and find out what the broader world of religion and spirituality had to say, what was the same, and what was different.

One thing I learned was that all of the major religions appear to almost oppose the concept of wealth (there's that money thing again). But I think this is often misunderstood. Christianity, for one, says that the problem is the love of money. As we've just discussed, one of the keys of a healthy relationship with money is to think of money as a tool, not as an end unto itself. Do you love the money, or do you love all the good you can do with it? It's hard to open an orphanage without some money. Just sayin'.

See how the relationships start to intertwine and influence each other? Your relationship with spirituality affects your relationship with money (and everything else). I won't talk about what sort of spirituality you ought to pursue—that's entirely up to you—just make sure you're doing it because it makes sense to *you* and not because you were raised that way or formed a particular belief years ago that no longer resonates or makes sense to you now. I know that's a hard pill for many people to swallow, but one of the greatest disservices we can do to ourselves is to let ourselves be shackled to beliefs and attitudes that were handed down to us by others. It's okay to free yourself from inherited baggage. Find what works for *you* and forge your own path.

CRITICAL RELATIONSHIP #3: YOUR RELATIONSHIPS WITH *OTHERS*

Our relationships with others should be examined just as rigorously as our relationships with money and spirituality. Each one's a little harder. Money is hard. Spirituality is harder and more personal. Now we're talking about *other people*, cranking the difficulty level up another notch.

But the difficulty isn't necessarily in the decision-making. Think about each of the people, individually, in your circle of friends.

What about your own coaches and peers in the trades? How do they make you feel? Do they raise your spirits, support you, console you, make you feel like you can take on the world and win? Or do they suck the life out of you, bring you down, burden you with troubles, and sap your energy? Obviously, I'm talking about extremes, and most of us are somewhere in between these, and we may shift from one end to the other depending on our current circumstances. The question is this: do you have "friends" who constantly wear you down while providing little positive benefit in return? If so, those are friends that, as harsh as it may sound, you might be better off without.

Here's the harder question: What kind of friend are *you*? Do you strive to uplift and support people? If you do, you can look forward to more in return. It doesn't mean you can't lean on a friend when bad things happen; that's what friends are for. But the overarching theme of a friendship should be *positive*. If it isn't, something is amiss.

Your relationships with others become even more important when you're in a leadership role. Are you supportive of your team? If you foster positive relationships with them, they, in turn, will foster positive relationships with others. You set the standard, and your example trickles down throughout the entire organization to team members, clients, and even vendors.

Rethink your relationships. Seek to bolster and strengthen those that are mutually beneficial, those that nourish and support you, and minimize or eliminate those that don't.

CRITICAL RELATIONSHIP #4: YOUR RELATIONSHIP WITH *YOURSELF*

It all comes down to this: What kind of relationship do you have with yourself? Who *were* you? What made you the person you are? This is another exercise in self-awareness, and it's one of the most productive. Think about your personality, opinions, conversational style, and character, then ask yourself how they developed and where they came from. With a little effort, you'll be able to see how you've been shaped by parents, siblings, teachers, and friends, which will make you more aware of how you're being influenced *now*. You may also discover a few traits that sprung solely from yourself alone.

Who *are* you? Are you happy with who you see when you look in the mirror? If there are traits that make you unhappy, that you don't like to think about, knowing where they came from can help you undo them and set things right. With self-awareness and massive effort, you can begin to rewire your programming and conditioning while becoming the person you wish to be.

Which brings us to the most important question of all: who will you *become*? You are always evolving; don't settle for who you are. Awareness of the *Relationships before Results* principle enables you to take control of your relationships and shape how your future unfolds. You can be the master of your own potential, freed from destructive influences that you've accumulated without even being aware of them. *Be aware.*

Of the four critical relationships (money, spirituality, others, and yourself), decide which one you'd like to improve right now. Write it down. Right here:

_____

On a scale of 1–10, how committed are you to making the necessary improvements?

_____

What is one action step you will take this week to help you improve this relationship?

_____

_____

_____

We are all influenced by attitudes and expectations of outside forces—many inherited from the past. Some of them work. Some of them almost certainly do not. We are captives to them, and we must forge our own identities and be aware of what we truly want. Your emotional freedom as a leader depends on it.

CHAPTER 6

LAW #3 PROBLEMS HOLD SOLUTIONS

THE PROBLEM WAS THAT I wasn't very good at school. In fact, I'm pretty sure the only comment on my report card one year was *DUMB KID*. And I believed that I was. I skated by with just above a D average, barely passing, absorbing the conventional wisdom that I just wasn't very smart. I did whatever I had to do to remain eligible for baseball, and that was it. Period.

Early in life, I knew that I was destined for a future of menial labor and minimum-wage jobs, which only convinced me that there was no point in trying. I fared no better in my one semester of college. No surprise, right? After all, my deficiencies had been well established. At least no one was disappointed. Heck, I only got accepted to college because I got a scholarship for my ability to play baseball better than most.

But then something amazing happened. I discovered that I had a tremendous work ethic and, even better, I could figure things out, I could diagnose problems and determine solutions, I could manage people and systems, I could make budgets and marketing plans, and I could actually run a drain cleaning company. This realization took time to understand and years to unlock. And then it hit me: I was *smart*! After a childhood of accepting the judgments of others, allowing them to damage my psyche, my self-image, and my self-worth, I finally realized that they had been wrong all along. The real problem was that I didn't like classrooms and homework, and I never learned to thrive in that environment. In fact, I believe to this day that the general school system simply didn't know how to effectively teach me the way I needed to learn (which is one reason I've committed my life and career to adult education).

As easy as it would be to gripe about the verdict that had been issued on my intelligence, my teachers had actually given me a tremendous gift: they had given me a huge problem that I had to overcome, and in the course of doing so, I learned more about myself in a few short years than I had in all of my previous existence. Could I have done that if they had told me how great I was and made things easy for me? I doubt it. And I can almost guarantee I would not be where I am today if I had left school with a clear path ahead of me.

BUT WHAT ABOUT EVERYONE ELSE?

I'm grateful for the hand I was dealt, and I am able to see, in retrospect, how it made me a better and more successful person. But I wonder how many people in situations similar to mine have had the opportunity to uncover this awareness and rewrite the script of their life. How many people in the trades have overcome the obstacles thrown in their way, have learned how to use them to become more than they might otherwise have been? How many people *haven't*? I wonder about all of the people who live their lives in ruts of their own making because they've failed to deal with problems and limitations that they've inherited, failed to identify, and failed to deal with. "I'm *just* a plumber." "I'm *just* a contractor." "I'm *just* a (fill in the blank)." These are lies. ALL LIES! You're so much more than that; it's time to understand and embrace your unique genius!

I know someone who managed a large lumber yard with over fifty employees. The staff was like a large family and overwhelmingly seemed to love their jobs, so it was heartbreaking when the company declared bankruptcy and began liquidating its assets. But the store closing had an important and unforeseen benefit: it forced those team members to question what they really wanted next as they moved on. The environment had been so welcoming and comfortable that few gave any thought to leaving. Some were settling for less than they truly desired in life and a career. In fact, many of them gave me a hard time when I honored my own truth and left to start my drain cleaning business several years before the company's downfall. Now, faced with unemployment and loss of income, they took what was, in many cases, a long-delayed next step. Many of my previous coworkers are now salespeople, home builders, tradespeople, consultants, business owners, and teachers, among other things.

If they hadn't been faced with a problem and forced to deal with it, most of them would probably still be happily stocking shelves with their friends.

I also know someone who got downsized from an executive position with an energy company. His position and experience should have made him instantly employable, or so you would think. He found out the hard way that most companies are not eager to hire people who are not good at selling themselves. After several months of flailing despair, he finally realized what an opportunity he had been given: he no longer *had* to work for someone else, but he had also never run his own business. As scary as that was, he threw himself into the challenge and leveraged his extensive knowledge and experience into creating a massively successful and very lucrative energy services business. He actually partnered with my accountant because he knew nothing about finance. The person that no one would hire now sets his own hours, works from wherever he likes, and earns a comfortable six figures using his own unique skillset, none of which would be true if he hadn't first been downsized and confronted with a problem that, at first, he seemed unable to overcome. In the end, he got creative and built a life far better than the one he lived before.

As for me, I was also backed into a corner. I did poorly in high school and dropped out of college. I got in trouble, went to jail, and ended up joining the army out of desperation for change. I didn't know what I was going to do, but I knew what I wasn't going to do, and that was any of the dead-end, physical, clock-punching jobs that seemed to be the only options open to someone in my position. Instead, as you know, I started my own business, which, while initially not tremendously successful, did put me on the path to the tremendous success that I enjoy today. If I hadn't been creative and aggressive about dealing with my perceived problem, I could still be sweeping the floor of a lumberyard instead of enjoying the sunset from a beach in Costa Rica with my wife, *the Lovely Christy*.

Sometimes we forget that the setback is actually the setup. Meaning, when life doesn't give you what you think you want, the world calls it a setback. However, when you look at your past, I believe you'll also see that most, if not all, of those "setbacks" were exactly what you needed to set you up for the next job, home, relationship, financial success, etc.

Years ago, a buddy of mine had a problem. He slipped on ice in a parking lot and cracked his head open. Fortunately, he was at a grocery store so there were people present to call an ambulance and have him rushed to the hospital. Upon further testing, the doctors found a tumor present in his skull growing next to his brain. They identified the tumor and removed it; he continued living a rewarding life. Had they not found the tumor, the diagnosis was certain to be fatal in a short period of time. This "problem" of falling and smacking his head was actually the "solution" to him staying alive!

I was raised in the Christian faith. People would say all the time that everything happens for a reason. As a kid, I was always fascinated by how quickly many people in the church would abandon this belief as soon as something happened specifically to them that wasn't to their liking. When someone else has a problem, it is pretty easy for us to say everything happens for a reason because what is happening is not happening to us. But how much does our belief get challenged when we have less-than-desired things happening in our own world? How does this show up in your own life and emotions?

I personally hold and live by a belief that all pain in the world is caused by not accepting what is—what is has already happened. We might not like it. We might not have chosen it, but it now *is*. As long as we resist what is happening or has happened, we will create pain for ourselves and those around us. This is a critical component of emotional regulation in leadership.

Do you believe life is happening *to you*, or is life happening *for you*? Think about this, contemplate this, and make a choice that will set you up for a new level of mental and emotional freedom. When you adopt the understanding that life is happening for you, all things in life simply become growth opportunities.

The point of all of the above is that successful people, and those who become purpose-guided leaders, learn how to break free of broken perspectives and limiting beliefs regarding problems. They learn to see problems as opportunities and they learn to understand that these opportunities happen *for* them, not *to* them. Virtually every one of the most successful people I know will tell you that they owe their position in life to a problem that they had to surmount.

THE PROBLEMS YOU SEE AND THE PROBLEMS YOU DON'T

The problems in the first two examples above have one thing in common: they were big problems thrust upon people by outside forces. Losing your job, suffering a debilitating injury, or having your car break down are all problems that are *obviously* problems. You know them when they happen and, one way or another, you're going to have to deal with them. This is where that shift in perspective becomes essential, and it's really very easy to do: "I lost my job, this is a new opportunity, and it might be scary, but I can now do something bigger and better than what I was doing before."

And yes, I know that's easier to say than it is to do. It can be a soul-crushing experience that makes you question everything about yourself. When one of my friends lost his job, I framed it as an opportunity and told him what a blessing it was to be able to begin a new and better chapter in his life. He replied, "Thanks. Can I be mad now?"

Yes, you can be mad. Take a day to grapple with your emotions, but don't dwell on them. That's the rut that so many of us slip into and, once you're in it, it can be hard to get out. Don't waste precious time ruminating over things that have already happened and can't be changed; instead, take that new perspective and start ruminating on the opportunities that lay before you. And that's the hardest part: you have to *force* yourself to do it when what you really want to do is curl up on the couch and feel sorry for yourself. Like I said, you have one day to feel sorry for yourself. Then it's time to get busy creating the life of your dreams.

Use your new self-awareness skills to cast problems in the light of opportunities. Every time you face a difficult issue, ask yourself how you can view it as a crossroads—there are multiple paths available. Which one will take you where you want to go?

What is one obvious problem you are facing right now that can be reframed into an opportunity?

_____

_____

_____

Now we come to the bigger issue and one that's infinitely more difficult to work with. When you lose your job, you know you have a problem (and an opportunity). It's kind of hard to miss. But you probably have problems you've been carrying around for years that you don't even know you have. Take my example from earlier in this chapter: I did poorly in school and dropped out of college, leaving me with lousy career options. Superficially, my problem was a lack of formal education, but on a deeper level, I was plagued by self-doubt and diminished self-worth because I had spent years being labeled *dumb*, and I was allowing that to hold me back and color what I thought I could do.

It took me a long time and a lot of coaching and counseling to get to the root of this issue and to learn how to use my experiences as an opportunity to help others in similar circumstances.

It took the self-awareness that comes with quieting my mind and focusing on my thoughts to really get at the root of it. It was a limiting belief and, after a lot of thought and self-examination, I was finally able to see it for what it was and mine it for the positive gifts it could provide. And that awareness came with a great side effect: I no longer look at my school years as a long, painful ordeal. I now see the massive gift I was given by not being able to learn effectively the way most of my classmates did. It's amazing what a little shift of perspective can do.

Examine your past for long-term problems that may be holding you back. Peel away the layers until you find the root of the issue, identify the growth opportunities, and use them to improve yourself, and cast any painful past experiences in a positive new light.

Do you still have that notebook or paper (probably need more paper by now)? Maybe you should grab a journal. Of all the problems you've experienced in your past, from childhood relationships to business challenges, what is still causing pain rather than feeling like a gift of life experience? What problems, and opportunities, are hidden away in your mind? What preconceived notions, prejudices, and attitudes are you carrying around inside of you? What criticisms and put-downs, possibly received decades ago, do you still hold close and allow to tie you down and hold you back? This is where the limiting beliefs that we've discussed that have hindered your progress can be turned around and harnessed to improve your life, your career, and your leadership abilities as you begin to use the skills you've learned in this book to help others.

Every problem is a key to the future, even the little ones. The daily issues that creep up at home and at work give you opportunities to learn new ways of doing things, new solutions for old problems, and maybe even chances to do things in interesting and innovative ways that could impact your life far beyond the consequences of whatever momentary trouble you face. As I said, every problem is a key to the future, and the more keys you have, the more doors you can open. Open doors are opportunities. Start collecting the keys.

At this point, you might be saying to yourself, "I thought this was a leadership book!" It is, and you'll begin to see how we've been building up to it in the next chapter.

CHAPTER 7

LAW #4 PURPOSE-GUIDED RESPONSIBILITY

YOUR TEAM MEMBERS ARE *not your friends. Don't get too close to your staff, or they'll take advantage of you. It's nothing personal; it's just business. The sole purpose of a business is to make a profit. If you don't hit the target, you are a failure as a leader.*

Do any of these sound familiar? Of course they do. I'll bet you've heard all of these. Maybe you even believe them. Running a company, managing a team, or being the head of a household is an act of stewardship that requires careful oversight of activities and plenty of leadership by example, but the old notion that only those with iron fists and cold hearts can succeed is simply not true. The most successful leaders are those who understand that their organizations, whatever they may be, are extensions of themselves.

LIMITING BELIEFS OF LEADERSHIP

The problem with most traditional leadership concepts—and I'm talking specifically about business leadership in home services—is that they transform people into nothing more than a means to an end. Companies love to say that their people are their most important assets, but too few treat them that way. Our business culture in the trades has increasingly grown toward sacrificing everything for the bottom line and eliminating anything—and anyone—that gets in the way.

Those companies do have one thing right, though: their people *are* their most important assets. It's time to start treating them that way, which requires moving beyond limiting beliefs of leadership. How many of these leadership limiting beliefs will you check off?

- ❑ **It's all about your bottom line.** I don't live in a self-improvement fantasyland where the bottom line doesn't matter. Of course it does, and it's crucial. Without a healthy bottom line, you will have difficulty keeping the wheels turning, and they may grind to a halt altogether. But—good or bad—it's your people who make it all happen.

- ❑ **It's all about your key performance indicators (KPIs).** KPIs are more likely to be your immediate benchmark than the bottom line if you're a manager. Your deliverables, efficiency ratings, margins, and ratios all depend on your greatest asset: your people.

- ❏ **It's all about your business valuation.** If you're an owner looking to sell your company, your business valuation will take center stage. The trouble is that your business valuation looks at your income statement, balance sheet, inventory, physical location, systems—basically everything *except* your people, who are almost treated as intangibles, even though absolutely nothing can happen without them.

- ❏ **It's all about task management and putting out fires.** Sadly, many leaders are so knee-deep in the minutiae of running their companies that they never tackle the larger issues that could lift them out of that swamp. The solution, of course, rests with the people who are already on the job being trained and led effectively. "Who" is always more important than "how" when it comes to building freedom, purpose, and profitability into an organization.

- ❏ **It's all about your people (but not in the way that you think).** Many owners and managers operate by suspicion: *Everyone is trying to rob, cheat, or steal. Everyone takes shortcuts when I turn my back. No one is loyal.* Bad things do happen—I'm sure you've heard stories—but you can be sure bad things will happen if you treat your team with constant suspicion.

I'm sure you can think of a few more limiting beliefs (feel free to write them down), but the five I listed illustrate my main point: home service businesses (regardless of size, location, or services offered) are all riddled with owners and managers who devalue people, even if subconsciously. The key to revolutionary leadership in the home service business is to put the value back where it belongs—on team member growth through effective training, coaching, and holding everyone accountable to their greatest selves.

PURPOSE-GUIDED RESPONSIBILITIES

Now it's time to bring your new self-awareness skills and personal responsibility to your business. Just as you strive to go beyond what society expects you to be, so must your business. What kind of culture do you want? One that people tell horror stories about, or one so awesome it makes recruiting virtually effortless? You've heard of both, I'm sure. Which do you want to be?

Your contracting business is ultimately an extension of your leadership ability. It's a reflection of your beliefs, what you want to accomplish, and your personal and professional education. I believe your business is also your creative outlet. So find that quiet place where you can slow your thoughts and really focus and then ask yourself: what kind of company do I truly want this to be?

Is it a company that stands only for the shallow accumulation of wealth? One that helps me bolster my ego? Or is it a one-of-a-kind contracting business that seeks to build better people and a stronger community while earning a healthy profit along the way?

I want to challenge you with a new way of thinking about your business. Whatever it is that you do—service and repair, add-on replacement, new construction, *anything*—if you have employees, a staff, a *team*, you are in the personal-development business. You're in business to make money so that you can do the *real business* of helping your people become the best individuals that they possibly can, better friends, better spouses, better parents, better *team members*. Take care of your team, and not only will your team take care of you, but the bottom line will also take care of itself.

Your responsibilities in this leadership revolution are making a profit *and* developing your team. Some of my clients hold in-house training about everything from successful relationships to parenting, eating healthier, and money management. In other words, they work to help them become all-around better people, which ultimately helps them become better team members. Imagine the positive impact you can make on your staff and their families and the positive impact that they, in turn, will make on others in their own circle of influence.

Many years ago, I hired Russ as an apprentice plumber. He was a line cook at a crappy restaurant in town and had no experience, at all, in the trades. One of my team members told him to come and talk to me as back then I was still doing the hiring at my service company. I liked him, he seemed like a good kid, so I gave him a chance. I, myself, certainly wasn't tremendously developed as a leader at that time, but I knew enough to know how to empower Russ to believe in himself like never before.

I showed him that I believed in him. I was willing to take a chance, invest, and place my confidence in him. He took it and ran with it, and watching him get married, buy a house, and have his beautiful little daughter on my watch is something I will always cherish.

Once, I was hired to moderate a father–son conversation in a family plumbing business. They were having a hard time communicating and were at a breaking point in their personal and business relationship. The son was a young and driven master plumber, and the father was an old-school master plumber who felt the younger generation weren't "paying their dues." After a full day of facilitation, we got clarity about the gap and helped them move forward in an aligned front, continuing to grow the business together with respect for each other's individual paths. As a leader, when you empower your team and allow them to have their own walk of success, they take that empowerment to every relationship in their lives, including other team members, as well as clients.

During the COVID-19 pandemic, one of my fastest-growing clients made some adjustments because they truly care about their people and the entire family unit of their team members. They identified how much hardship the pandemic was creating for their team members who had young children and didn't know what to do with them when things were shut down and difficult to navigate. My client Mike stepped to the plate and converted the company's training room into a daycare, took the legal steps necessary to hire the right people, and "put his money where his mouth is" regarding his genuine care for his team and their families. His team loves working for this business; they refer friends and family to work at this business, helping them remain in growth mode, which is a tremendous positive by-product of exemplifying great leadership in a challenging time.

When you're clear about your purpose and live in alignment with it, you can rest assured it will shape your company's culture. When you bring your own purpose-guided leadership mindset into the workplace, the people around you will be able to tell. They'll see that there's something different about you. You will radiate a sense of peace and direction that those caught in life's tangle of day-to-day drudgery rarely achieve. Your team will notice. And they will want to emulate you and learn to live the same way. You can help them get there. For additional help discovering your own purpose, go to *www.BlueCollarBook.com* and grab my purpose-clarifying exercise.

This brings me to an important point: as a home services leader, people will be influenced by your behavior, good or bad, whether you realize it or not. If you radiate negativity, it will grow like a weed throughout your organization. Be mindful of your speech, behavior, and tone when speaking. Being a leader makes you larger than life, whether you realize it or not. Be the person that you want everyone else to be.

What specific changes could you make to have a more positive impact through your leadership role and responsibilities? Use that journal or notebook if you need more space.

MIX WITH THE MASSES

Successfully developing your people means spending time with them. If you already do that, great. But if you're more of an office-dweller, it may be time to circulate a little. There's plenty you can do to set a positive example from afar, but you need to be visible and approachable to be truly effective. Just as you are being observed, you can also observe the people keeping your company going. What you do on a holistic, company-wide scale can—and should—also be accomplished person-to-person. Take a personal interest in your team member's well-being, from the personal to the professional. It's good to know how the people in the trenches perceive working conditions and training programs, but it's equally good to know how things are going at home.

Domestic challenges can have a massive effect on job performance, which is one reason why the companies that really do well with this sort of approach offer the personal-development programs that I mentioned a few paragraphs ago. When things run smoothly at home, they run smoothly at work, and vice versa. The company's influence extends into the home and, conversely, the workplace becomes an extension of the family.

Building a loving team with true empathy depends upon the development of every person. Put on a uniform, get in a truck and do a ride-along. Attend a weekly training meeting. Sit in the call center for an afternoon. Get out of your comfort zone as a leader. You'll be amazed by what you'll learn, and the personal connections you'll enjoy will be invaluable.

Consistency is key, one action, one lesson, one team member at a time. The way you do one thing is the way you do everything. This is what separates those who are in touch with their own purpose from those who try to project normalcy and calm while chaos stirs inside them. Those who haven't calmed their own thoughts will inevitably slip and reveal their inner turmoil, showing flashes of anger, impatience, and selfishness. I know; I've been there. One such mistake can damage your ability to set a positive example in ways that can take months, even years, to rectify. The solution: quiet your thoughts, learn to understand yourself, discover your true responsibility as a leader, and live your life with purpose.

One challenging area we repeatedly see regarding walking with the masses shows up in the middle-level management roles. Oftentimes, these managers were promoted from the field or call center into a manager title and role. Because of this, an individual operating largely from the subconscious mind can allow ego to enter the equation and feel a sense of entitlement as a manager. They can feel and display behavior evidencing they are now somehow "better" than the frontline team, where they came from.

You must address and discuss this with middle-level managers. If you are reading this and you are a middle-level manager, ask yourself a couple of questions: *When was the last time I did frontline work with my team? When was the last time I did a ride-along (or a desk-along) and actually performed the task(s) I require others to do?* For many managers in this role, it's been far too long. It's easy to lose connection to the team because one of the driving factors of becoming a manager is no longer *having* to perform those tasks.

Now I'm not saying managers need to get back in the trenches full-time, but for respect to remain present, it's crucial that frontline team members know and feel that managers are no better than they are. This is a vital distinction many managers miss regarding the difference between confidence and self-worth. Confidence has to do with a specific skill. Self-worth has to do with how someone values themself. Just because a manager is skilled at a particular part of a job, they are not better people than those who report to them.

Get involved with your team. Physical involvement is not always the answer. Sometimes a simple phone call or text message with genuine empathy, care, or concern is all the team needs to feel included and truly valued by a manager. Which of these areas do you think you could improve?

An organization that transcends KPIs and the bottom line is one that is built for success and influence that reaches far beyond its intended footprint and impacts the community around it. Be the leader everyone wants to follow; build the company everyone wants to work for. Embrace your purpose-guided responsibilities, and your influence can last for generations.

CHAPTER 8

LAW #5 CANDID COMMUNICATION

EVERYONE DREADS THE MEETING. *I avoid one-on-ones like the plague. I feel like I have to walk on eggshells around Sarah. I get so tired of Sam repeating the same thing over and over without ever actually saying anything. No one ever gets what I'm trying to say. Jay misinterpreted another email. This business would be great if it weren't for all the sparring with team members and clients!*

Ever feel like you're a professional babysitter? You're not alone, and the solutions will impact every area of your life and business. Let's fix this and finally set you free.

But first, there's something that we need to talk about.

LIMITING BELIEFS ABOUT COMMUNICATION

- **Intimidation is influence.** Think about the stereotypical "boss" that you see in TV shows and movies. Whether they're blowhards or smooth-talking managers, in most cases, their methods of communication with subordinates involve some form of intimidation, ranging from outright yelling and ranting to subtle insinuations and veiled threats. I'm sure you've been on the receiving end of someone like this at some point in your life. How effective were they as communicators? Did they leave you wanting to do your best, or did they leave you wanting to bolt for the door?

- **Everyone understands what I mean.** If you've ever asked someone to do something only to find out later that they did something very different from what you had in mind, whose fault is that? Sure, maybe the person is really bad at following instructions. Or maybe you weren't as clear as you thought you were. I've found from working with hundreds of progressive contractors that the latter is almost always the case. Communicating for clarity and understanding by everyone involved is an art that you must master.

- **If I say something that upsets someone, that's *their* problem.** Again, you may be dealing with someone who looks for things to get upset about, but that doesn't describe most people. If you're in a position of authority, it is incumbent upon you to think before you speak, especially in today's business climate where leaders are often held accountable for what may have seemed an innocent slip of the tongue. Remember that one person's idea of a harmless joke is another person's idea of harassment. Personally, I'm not big on being too "politically correct," and I'm certainly what most consider a nonconformist. However, I must respect everyone's personal reality without judgment. Whether I actually agree or not with their view is a moot point; I'd rather win the game we're playing in business together than be right about some socioeconomic view or religious perspective.

THE SOLUTION IS SELF-AWARENESS

By now, you should be sensing a theme. As with so many other things, the key to success in communication is greater self-awareness. How do you like people to talk to you? What assumptions do you make when you speak with others? Do you provide all the information necessary for someone to follow your instructions, or do you leave out things that might be common knowledge to you but a complete mystery to others? When you slow down your thoughts and think deeply, ask yourself how you come across to others. If you're honest, there's about a fifty–fifty chance you won't like the answer. The good news is that a little self-awareness can solve this issue.

Here's an example: if you are in any sort of supervisory position, from department manager to company owner, anyone who reports to you will be at least a little intimidated by your position no matter how hard you try to compensate for it with kindness and understanding. It just comes with the territory. I try to build a unified, connected front by referring to my company's employees as team members. We are all in this together. Yet, no matter how hard I try, I am still the boss, and I know I'm still seen that way. The same is true for anyone in a position of authority: your subordinates are unlikely to be completely at ease when you're around. If you tell someone they did a good job, your praise will be magnified by virtue of your position. Likewise, a scold, even a mild one, could land with far more impact than you ever intended. While there may never be a way to erase this (after all, you're still in charge), simple awareness of how people feel can go a long way toward improving communication.

With that in mind, on some level, I think we all know that yelling at someone isn't the way to get what you want in the long run, but especially not if you're yelling at a subordinate. Shouting in anger may produce immediate results, but it's also the surest way to make your team member consider looking for a new job alongside anyone else who saw it happen. I know this all too well from my own previous experience.

Anger and impatience are real. We've all been there. I once encountered an advertising salesperson who told me he could run a local direct-mail campaign for my company, reaching 60,000 unique homes per quarter. The trouble is, I already knew that the local market I serviced only contained about 33,000 homes. Instead of asking questions for additional clarity or help with understanding the math, I lost my mind and threw him out of my office. I used to feel a short-term win from "being right" in situations like these. But in the long run, I always felt terrible afterward, and it took some time for me to recover, time that I could have spent doing something much more productive. *Candid Communication* and communicating only to prove a point are two vastly different approaches, which yield very different results. Communicating from a place of anger or "being right" always ends in disappointment. It can forever alter a relationship, and it can make you—and other people—feel awful.

How do *you* react to angry communication? Does it fill you with the urge to cooperate, to make things happen, to go the extra mile? Or does it make you defensive, fill you with resentment, and only do what's required to make the problem go away?

When you feel anger swell up inside you, take a moment to cool down before talking. The old adage of counting to ten before speaking is still good advice, but go one step further: always assume that there may be more to the issue than you know. It would be a shame to ruin someone's day and sabotage a team member's attitude only to find out that the issue was the product of a misunderstanding. This brings us to the fact that you can't communicate effectively with others until you can communicate effectively with yourself (more self-awareness).

Most people don't understand their own issues and desires. I used to have no idea how much my own issues, challenges, and conditioning (from as far back as childhood) affected me as a leader. They motivate us, restrain us, steer us, tell us what to say and do, and yet we don't know what they are, and, worse, we don't even *know* that we don't know. Unless, that is, you practice the type of self-awareness that we discussed earlier in this chapter. When it comes to communication, having that understanding will put you head and shoulders above those who don't. The root of successful communication is understanding. How can you understand others if you don't understand yourself?

When you understand your innermost self, you'll be better able to do the same for—and more importantly, empathize with—other people. You'll see the same hopes and fears, the same confidence and insecurity, and you'll be able to relate to them on a far deeper level than if you had, as most people do, a shallower self-understanding. Understanding yourself gives you a baseline for understanding others. It's like being an airplane pilot: you can fly without understanding the underlying science, but you might hit the ground. You'll be a far better pilot if you *do* understand. So seek to understand. Connect with yourself before you connect with others.

How do you know when it's enough? You don't. And you'll never stop changing. You're not the same person now as you were last year, and you'll be a different person again twelve months from now, which means that you can never stop working to understand yourself. It's a never-ending process. And, to the best of your ability, you have to work to understand your team members in the same way. Spend time with them. Learn about what motivates them, their fears and desires, what makes them tick. Then you will truly begin to communicate on a higher level.

When was the last time you had a conversation where you lost your temper or ended up feeling your blood pressure *and voice* rising out of control during the communication? Who was the conversation with? What was it about? How did it make you feel?

_____

_____

_____

_____

Reacting to situations is one area in which we often lose control of our emotions, which automatically lowers our ability to communicate at the highest level. Now that you've thought through the scenario above, knowing what you now know, what could you have done differently before and during the conversation? Be as honest and specific as possible.

_____

_____

_____

_____

SO MUCH TO COMMUNICATE

It's too bad this whole book isn't about communication because we could talk about it forever. That's why there *are* whole books dedicated to the topic. In these pages, I'm focusing on the aspects that I think are most important to the home service leadership revolution, but by all means, learn all you can about communication. In the meantime, here are a few more thoughts.

- **Strive for a sense of unconditional love in communication.** Everyone should know that, even if they'd rather not hear it, what they're told is coming from a place of love, that it's said with the goal of helping them to grow, to become a better person, parent, spouse, or team member.

- **Don't make assumptions based on past interactions.** No two people are alike. Of course, you already know this, but we sometimes forget when it comes to working with others. Just because something works with one person doesn't mean it will work with another. People are individuals, and each one requires customization. Use what you know about yourself and them to communicate on their levels in the most effective ways.

- **Don't take things emotionally.** Negative emotional reactions are the root of pain for most bad interactions. Feelings get hurt, offenses are taken, and those effects linger long after the conversation has ended. Remember that, especially in the workplace, it's rarely about *you*. Half of the responsibility in every interaction is striving to receive information and understand things as intended. Don't assume that everything comes across exactly the way you intend. If you feel uneasy for any reason, ask questions for additional clarity to minimize uncertainty and negative emotions.

- **Don't assume that you are understood.** This is the flipside to the previous point. Don't assume that what you say is absorbed and properly understood. Especially as a leader, you will find that some of the people you speak with will act as if they understand everything perfectly regardless of whether or not they actually do. Ask questions. Find out if they grasp what you are trying to say. If they don't, clarify. Failure to understand is a two-way street; both sides have a job to do. Nothing clears the air like asking for clarity, and it's a great way to make a connection because it shows that you truly care.

- **Digital communication requires special attention.** This is a bit of a left turn for this chapter, but it's important: remember that unless you're on video, recipients can't see your facial expressions or hear your tone of voice. It's too easy for your intentions to be misinterpreted and misunderstood. When composing emails and text messages, it's best to keep things neutral and to the point. The last thing you want to have to do is send a follow-up email that says, "I WAS KIDDING!" I once utilized software that required calls to be booked in the system by typing in all capital letters. If my CSRs didn't change the "all caps" setting, they would send me, and even clients, emails in all caps, and it always felt like they were yelling!

Think about how you feel after a great conversation. You're happy, you feel understood, you have a spring in your step, and you're ready for whatever comes next. This is what candid communication can help you and your team experience every single day.

CHAPTER 9

LAW #6 ALIGNED ACCOUNTABILITY

UNLESS YOU'RE A SADIST (or a masochist), you probably don't enjoy having to "write someone up." Of course, it is occasionally necessary, but it isn't pleasant for either party. And when it comes to overall performance and accountability, there can be an annoyingly wide spectrum of gray areas: *Jim is a great installer and does spectacular work, but he's always late. Suzy shows improvement in her appointment booking rate, but she's nowhere close to what we agreed upon for company minimums. Doug is our best salesperson, but he's also a bit of a loose cannon.* Wouldn't it be great if everyone could get on the same page and be aligned a little more closely in their workplace activity and outlook?

Everyone *can*. And when they are, your whole business will run much more smoothly, and write-ups will be few and far between.

Getting everyone on the same page isn't as much about one-on-one communication (although that always plays a role) as it is about influence, and influence relies upon the influencer's self-acceptance. The more you're in touch with yourself, your goals, and your desires, the easier it is to get others to buy into them. I'm sure you've encountered people who aren't fully on board with their stated ambitions. They're shaky. They're unsure. It may not be obvious, but on some level, even subconsciously, you can tell that something is amiss. These people face an uphill battle when it comes to influence.

Get rock solid with yourself and make sure you are truly convinced of your purpose before attempting to convince others to follow you. If you still feel unsure, go back now and spend some time getting it right. It's important for what comes later. Then take a few moments, and ask yourself if you feel like there is any misalignment between your purpose as a leader and your company mission. If so, think about (and use that journal or notebook to write down) what actions you can take to remedy the situation.

LIMITING BELIEFS OF ALIGNED ACCOUNTABILITY

Collective consciousness in business has often taught us a limiting belief that accountability is supposed to be a fight—an "us and them" mentality, where we are like tennis players on opposite ends of the court trying to win a match. (For more on the "us and them" mentality, please read or listen to my book *The Six Dimensions of C.H.A.N.G.E. 2.0.*)

This is an incredibly destructive leadership belief to allow. You and your team are united in your goals. You all want the same end result. You want to win together. The only way that happens is when you all (you and your team) take full responsibility for your own individual contributions to the desired goal. This is when aligned accountability really begins to work.

Conversely, relationships are damaged when we hold on to the belief that I, as the leader, must *forcefully* hold my direct report accountable to be better at (whatever the key performance indicator is), as well as the beliefs that because of this, we must have "difficult" conversations, I may have to "write (them) up," and we are not going to get along during this process. As a result, trust is lost. Empathy is gone. Collaboration gets thrown out the window.

Instead, focus on setting the goal (or missed goal) on one side of the tennis court, so to speak, and you and your direct report begin acting like you're playing doubles together in order to overcome your shared opponent—the result that is not being met.

One limiting belief about accountability is that it should focus on small things, like compliance, timeliness, performance results, sales targets, etc. You get the picture. All of these are vitally important, but there's a way to get many of these small issues to take care of themselves. When team members feel micromanaged on every level, they start believing they can never satisfy you as a manager. Make sure they understand why you must have the small things (mentioned above) followed and adhered to, and you're simply there to support them, help them, and make it as easy as possible for them to perform their jobs in a winning manner.

THE MAGIC OF A SHARED VISION

Think about the one-on-one communication addressed in the last chapter. As you strive to build those connections with your team members, it's also vital to connect the members of your team to your company's overarching vision, whatever it may be. I don't cover mission and vision statements in this book, but if you have one, now is a good time to get it out to review. If you don't have one, I highly encourage you to invest the time and energy in the process of creating a meaningful mission statement that you and your team can rally around. (Please feel free to reach out to us at the Blue Collar Success Group for any assistance in the process of discovering your mission, vision, purpose, or values).

Communicate your company's mission to your team. Maybe it's to dominate your market, do the most good for the most people, be the most innovative company in the entire industry, or develop your team into the very best people they can be. Whatever it is, communicate it to your team with the massive enthusiasm and certainty that comes with true self-awareness and belief in your own cause. Your mission is worthless unless your people buy into it; there is no room for doubt here. For example, at the Blue Collar Success Group, our mission is to accelerate the path of success for home service companies. Period.

Everything we do all day, every day, is geared around this simple yet profound mission. From the time a team member joins us, they understand, embrace, and execute our company mission.

When your company's mission is clearly communicated and understood, you've taken a huge step in the right direction, but the real work is just beginning. As far as your people are concerned, grasping the big picture is one thing; understanding their roles in the master plan is something else. It is imperative that each individual team member understands his or her role in the success of the mission in real, concrete terms. All of this is obvious when you're the leader at the top, but when you're somewhere below that level, it's easy to feel like you're a cog in a mysterious machine that serves no definable purpose.

When your team buys into the mission, and when they understand how what they do contributes to the overall operation, how it helps other team members do their jobs, how it augments the overall well-being of the organization, and how it helps ensure their own security and prosperity, then they stop thinking like employees working for a paycheck and start thinking like members of a coordinated organization that strives toward a common, achievable, beneficial goal. It's a shift of mindset that will make deep and far-reaching changes to your company. It's not me, and it's not you. It's *us*. It's energizing, it's invigorating, it's propulsive, it's inspiring, and it completely changes the way accountability works.

How can achieving a shared vision help to overcome the particular issues that your organization faces?

One example is a client we have in Denver. He used to work his team to the brink of insanity, but a few years ago, he embraced this concept of a shared vision. He was operating from a place with no emotion and a mindset that was based on, "I'm paying them to do a job; what else do they need?" Once he understood the damage he was inflicting with that mindset and method of communication, he changed his actions around (and feelings about) his team. Now, he constantly shares where the company is going as a whole and how they are all going to achieve this success together. This company has become an industry-leading juggernaut in a very short period of time, consistently setting records for sales, average tickets, and profits.

Another good example is a plumbing company in Chicago that was struggling with their culture due to offering twenty-four-hour service when they only had a few trucks to cover all the after-hours work. They had a shared vision meeting with the team and listened empathically to the genuine concerns negatively impacting families, sleep, and ultimately, their overall performance even during normal business hours. After working through a great communication process, the decision was made to increase the fees for after-hours work and only offer it to service-agreement customers. This improved morale so much that the company was able to add a few more trucks rather quickly and ultimately eliminate the shortage issue for the on-call schedule.

Let me just expose a potential limiting belief you might be feeling right now. Did you read that last story and feel any negative emotions? Are you potentially "old school," and you cannot possibly believe a company would change its customer service plans based on what team members said or wanted? Welcome to the new world of the service business, my friend! Your number one customer is your internal customer—your immediate team. Sure, when I started back in 1994, I was by myself in a truck and on-call 24/7, 365 for two solid years. Guess what? Nobody cares. That was then; this is now. Shared vision and great communication create aligned accountability.

AN ACCOUNTABILITY REVOLUTION

Now that your team is on board with your company's mission, accountability starts to look very different. Instead of holding people to task for the nuts and bolts of their daily jobs, now you're holding them accountable for an essential role in a much larger purpose. Earlier in this book, I mentioned the mindset of someone who lived through World War II on the home front: *How is what I am doing right now helping to win the war?* Now, with an understanding of the company's mission and purpose, your team also has a war to win. If everyone understands their role, is enthusiastic about the mission, and grasps how their jobs impact their teammates, most of the petty issues that used to plague your day-to-day operations will slip away. Everything becomes about the team and its shared purpose. Accountability (and performance reviews) become functions of how the group is doing as a whole and how the individual's contribution helps (or doesn't).

This doesn't mean that you'll never have to have the occasional candid communication session for clarity or refocusing responsibilities, but there will be fewer of them, and they will absolutely take on a different energy. But if you're compassionate in your authority (as I hope you are), you might find yourself challenged by one of the same issues as before: the better you know your people, the harder it can be to hold them accountable.

Think about it: the closer you get to your team, the more your team feels like family, and if you have a family, you're probably familiar with the concept of letting things slide. Your affection and love for your children gets in the way of discipline, and whichever problem you're avoiding rarely takes care of itself. *Emotion is the accountability blocker.* Don't let your feelings get in the way of aligned accountability because, just like your children, sparing your team members the experience will only cause them—and your team—to pay a higher price later.

Is that journal or notebook close by? What persistent accountability problems has *your* business faced? Do the same problems keep coming up? Do you have "repeat offenders"?

I remember having issues getting a previous general manager of mine to focus on what mattered most. He was a shiny-object guy, and I came to realize that without specific tasks or guidelines to keep him focused, he simply didn't know what he should be doing to leverage his time and expertise to help grow the business. At first, I would get super frustrated, ask him why he was or wasn't doing certain things, etc. The issue would resurface every few months, and it began to drive me crazy. I knew he was a good manager. I knew he cared about the business. I knew he wanted to do well. I just wasn't providing him great feedback and holding him accountable to the action plan. This is a dangerous place many entrepreneurs like me find ourselves. Because as a driven entrepreneur, I don't necessarily want a specific path or daily plan to follow; I hesitate to hold high-level management accountable to specific plans as well.

The solution I found, in this case, was implementing a periodical and unannounced shadowing day for my GM. On this day, I would just randomly show up first thing in the morning and advise him I would "be in his pocket" for that entire day, observing and taking notice of how he spent his time. I would not do any coaching or correcting of behavior or time management during the observation day at all. (This is not easy to do, but critically important; the entire goal of this process is to see how time and resources are being deployed daily without your involvement.)

The following day we would have out-of-office coffee or lunch scheduled, and I would ask clarifying questions about phone calls, meetings, activities, and how he was thinking about certain things as he made on-the-spot decisions throughout the previous day. Then, and only then, would I offer a few items of observation or advice for him to reinforce effective actions and behaviors, as well as a few areas of identified improvement. Implementing this activity, which I would perform about once a quarter, was a game-changer for him as a manager, for the business results, and for our own relationship with each other. At first, it was very challenging for him because he felt put on the spot and felt like I was there to almost catch him doing something wrong. Once we developed an agreed understanding that my presence was truly coming from a place of love and support, and my feedback and demeanor demonstrated and proved that, we both got a tremendous amount of value from this activity. He got to see blind spots he was unaware of, and I got to perform incredibly effective coaching for the highest manager in my business. This is one of the most important roles of self-accountability for you to serve the other managers and leaders around you.

Keep in mind, just as your team members are accountable to you, you are accountable to your people. You are accountable for providing a safe and equitable workplace, for providing the tools and the knowledge that they need to do their jobs well and to meet your standards and, most importantly, for holding up your end of the bargain when it comes to fulfilling the company's mission. You are the guiding star, the driving force, and your team will only be as enthusiastic about it as you are. It's a never-ending job, and why would you want it any other way? How accountable are you really? Ready to find out? Utilize my accountability self-assessment at *www.BlueCollarBook.com*.

You are also accountable for the standards that you set for yourself and for everyone else. There is tremendous power in leading by example. Be the person you want everyone else to be, and your team will emulate your qualities. Don't mistake this for being perfect; it's NEVER about being perfect. It's simply about being authentic in who you are and what you're asking of those around you.

Just as I shared the story about my previous GM having "shiny object syndrome," I have the same challenge within my own leadership DNA. In fact, on the Kolbe A Index Instinctive Strengths Assessment, I score a nine out of ten in the "Quick Start" category and a two out of ten in the "Follow Through" category. I love to develop new ideas, get them started, and then I lose interest. I must be very clear with myself and my team about these strengths. Notice I said strengths, not weaknesses. I used to feel my lack of follow-through was a weakness. Now, after a lot of soul searching, coaching, and true understanding of what my mentor and coach Dan Sullivan refers to as Unique Ability, I know that all I have are strengths; I simply need to surround myself with team members that excel in areas that I'm not best cut out for.

When left unnoticed, unhonored, or unowned, these types of situations can become damaging to other managers as well as the business. We don't need to be perfect; we need to be honest, open, and vulnerable with our strengths and areas in which we need another team member to step up. When we don't hold ourselves accountable to "own our stuff," we can come off wanting people to do what I say, not what I do. We lose the authenticity of our truth, which is not loving or healthy to ourselves or anyone else. When I step into sharing my truth, whether it's perceived originally by the team as a strength or weakness, it always creates a communication and accountability platform of authenticity in a safe environment. It encourages everyone on the team to operate in the same manner. Honor your truth and hold yourself accountable while you continue to learn and grow as a leader in the organization.

Regardless of the current state of accountability within your organization, aligning your entire team with your mission will not only revolutionize your relationship with your people—it will also improve the way they go about their daily tasks.

CHAPTER 10

LAW #7 ESSENTIAL SELF-CARE

YEARS AGO, I HAD THE good fortune to see the legendary Zig Ziglar speak live. He asked the audience a question that stuck with me for the rest of my career: "If you had a million-dollar racehorse, would you treat it the same as a ten-dollar dog or a five-dollar cat?" Of course, you wouldn't. I know what you might be thinking—*of course* you would still love that dog and cat—but the racehorse, which has tremendous value beyond being a pet and companion, would probably (and justifiably) receive top-notch medical care, a special diet, regular training and exercise, and attention from experts and specialists.

And the fact that the racehorse cost a fortune isn't even the foremost reason to take such special care of it. The foremost reason to take care of the racehorse is because of what it can do for you in the future. It can earn many times its purchase price if you give it the appropriate care and attention. It's a valuable asset and, if you're smart, you'll treat it like one.

My friend, you are your own most valuable asset, and you are the most important value driver for yourself, your family, your company, and all of the team members who rely upon your guidance and leadership. You owe it to them—and yourself—to take impeccably good care of *you*.

THOSE PESKY LIMITING BELIEFS

One last time—start checking in on your limiting beliefs and take a look to really expose how your self-talk conversations are shaping up. When you talk negatively to yourself, you are speaking truth into the universe that you are not good enough, not worthy, and not ready for the success you are outwardly attempting to create. You spend more time talking to yourself than anyone else. Do yourself a favor and start talking to yourself like a best friend. You are an incredible leader, doing the very best you can. You continue to educate yourself (you're still reading this book, aren't you?), and you are committed to next levels of your own greatness. Only when you feel worthy will you be able to break through the collective limiting beliefs society holds regarding self-care. Some of these are listed below.

- **Self-care is optional.** This is an accepted and incredibly destructive belief to hold. I can certainly relate, as I used to feel this was true. Until I realized that all positive results in my life directly correlated to how well I treat myself, my mind, my body, and my divine relationship with my maker, I struggled. Now that I understand and execute from a place of "nothing is more important than my own self-care," I can live a life filled with ease, joy, and glory while balancing emotional regulation at a level I only used to dream of.

- **You should be ashamed.** While going to the gym is generally encouraged, many other self-care activities are often seen as frivolous and silly time-wasters. Some people are embarrassed by things like yoga classes, spiritual retreats, journaling, meditating, etc., and they seek to keep them hidden from others. And God forbid you go out for a massage. You sure wouldn't want your peers to know about *that*! Yet, these are exactly the kinds of self-care rituals that we need to be regularly doing and encouraging others to do as well. We'd all be happier, healthier, and more productive if we did.

- **It's a waste of time.** Who has the time? You're busy, right? You get in early, work all day on wall-to-wall projects, and when you get home (whenever that may be), you have to do prep work for the following day. It never lets up. The last thing on your mind is stuff that's just for *you*. The fact is you can't afford *not* to take the time. Your mental and physical health depend on taking time for yourself. If you think you're okay without taking the time, trust me: you'll be a hundred percent better if you do. In fact, you WILL make the time to take care of your health at some point in your life. You'll do it now in the way I'm suggesting, or you'll do it later in doctors' offices, hospitals, and requiring home care. I'm not trying to be harsh, but this point must not be taken lightly. It is a massive concern in our industry, and it's time to wake up!

- **It's a poor allocation of resources.** As previously stated, there are simply no sustainable resources without a consistent and effective self-care ritual. Time seems to be the resource we are challenged by the most when it comes to honoring a self-care ritual program. I believe you will make time for your health, now or later. Your mental wellness, your physical well-being, and your spiritual and divine connections will all have a time in life when they become a priority. The tragedy is that most of society waits until it's too late to honor and take care of business in these areas. If you believe you don't have the resource of time to meditate consistently, you will most likely develop emotional trauma at a level that will eventually manifest as disease. If you accept the false belief that you don't have time to eat sensibly or read/listen to good information daily, you will make time in the future by needing tests, doctor visits, and possible hospital stays. I'm not trying to be dramatic here, but I truly want you to understand how important this is!

- **Self-care is selfish.** I understand you might feel a twinge of guilt about it initially, but, like so many other things, it's only because our social and workplace environments have conditioned us to think that way. There's nothing selfish about a self-care routine that ultimately benefits not just you but everyone who lives and works with you. You might want to read that sentence again. Then you might want to program it into your subconscious mind to help set you free from limiting beliefs around what it takes to be a successful leader!

Self-care isn't optional, it isn't a waste of time, it isn't a poor allocation of resources, it isn't selfish, and it's nothing to be ashamed of. On the contrary: self-care is *essential*. Everyone who depends on you needs you to be in good health, mentally and physically. You are your company's North Star, and the North Star needs to be constant and sure. So take care of yourself. I have a five-point self-care ritual that works for me. It might work for you, too. I call it *The Five M's of Self-Care*.

THE FIVE M'S OF SELF-CARE

The First M: MEDITATE/PRAY. Your spiritual and psychological well-being are always of top importance. If you don't take the time to sort your thoughts and make peace with your daily mental clutter, you'll find yourself with so many things knocking around in your head that you won't be able to make sense of the chaos. You might think that you're okay, that you don't need it, that watching a little TV in the evening is just as good a way to unwind as meditation. Here's the thing: meditation isn't about unwinding. Unwinding may be a fringe benefit, but meditation is really about winding things *differently*.

Throughout the course of the day, we're bombarded by things that we can't manage or control. This can range from the minor "Truck number fourteen needs brakes again because of Mike's driving!" to the major "The warehouse is on fire!" to the mundane "Jimmy was late to school!" When we're in the middle of all this activity, the best we can hope to do is take action when action is needed, leaving the mental fallout for later. All of that piles up in your head, distracting and sidetracking you, buzzing around like angry bees in the back of your mind even when you don't realize it.

Meditation can help straighten all of that out. As discussed earlier in this book, you can slow down and quiet your thoughts through meditation. Then, when you're at peace and able to focus, go over your day, focusing on the high points and the low, and when the events that caused trouble and stress cross your mind, seek to put them to rest. If the problem is resolved, then resolve the lingering thoughts. Make a conscious effort to put them aside. It's over; don't dwell on it. If it isn't resolved, now is the time to focus your thoughts on a solution. Even the most panic-inducing issues seem smaller and more manageable through the lens of meditation.

I use meditation as a catch-all term because it can apply to everyone, but prayer can be equally important. Seeking the guidance of a higher power is also a powerful way to put your mind at ease and productively focus your thoughts on what's ahead.

Meditation helps you make sense of the world around you, helps you sort out the activities of your day, and helps you clean the slate for the next morning. It also helps you feel better physically. The mind has a powerful hold on our moods, and our moods influence how we feel. Likewise, your body can affect your moods. And this brings us to the next M.

The Second M: MOVE. If your mind feels run down, the problem is probably partly physical, and if your body feels run down, the problem is probably partly mental. In other words, your body and mind are tightly bound together and what affects one affects the other.

Exercise if you want to. Go to the gym and work out if you like. But movement can be as simple as taking a walk around the block. It can be doing ten burpees in your living room or doing a yoga program (which often has the added benefit of including meditation). Anything that gets the joints and the muscles going qualifies and will make you feel better and more alive, even if you felt pretty good to begin with.

It's essential to keep movement at the forefront of your self-care routine. Don't neglect it. As we gain more responsibilities in life and business, a sad fact for many of us is that we spend more time staring at a computer screen, with the physical workout confined to our fingers. Get up and move! The health benefits of even the simplest exercise are well documented. And you might just find that you do your best thinking when you're walking. The movement, the fresh air, and the changing scenery will stimulate your mind in ways that sitting in front of a computer never will.

The Third M: MIND DOWNLOAD. Journaling is the active counterpart to meditation and prayer. After you've gained clarity and peace with your thoughts, take a few minutes to record them in a journal. You can use anything from a plain wire-bound notebook to an elaborate blank book sold in bookstores and stationery departments. Regardless, make sure you're doing it in a way that can be kept together and preserved.

Can you journal on a computer? Sure. I have plenty of clients that do electronic journaling. But I encourage you to try journaling longhand with pen and paper. Writing longhand engages your mind in ways that keyboarding does not, and you'll find yourself thinking in ways that differ from any other activity. The act of holding the pen, of writing on paper, the sound of the point dragging across the surface, leaving a trail of ink, becomes a sort of meditation unto itself, warmer and more intimate than the cold digital light of a computer monitor. Try it.

Don't simply record the events of the day. This isn't as much about keeping a record as it is about *thinking*. Write down your thoughts and opinions; express your feelings, good and bad. As you do, something amazing will happen. You'll begin to think of things that wouldn't have occurred to you if you hadn't been writing. Your perspective and opinions will clarify, your ideas will crystallize, and you'll gain insights and a maturity of thought that elude those who don't take the time to analyze their own thinking. It's a great quality to cultivate and a great advantage to have.

The Fourth M: MENTAL FOOD. They say, *You are what you eat*, and the same goes for what you feed your mind. I can't emphasize enough the importance of keeping yourself on a diet of positive, uplifting, and educational media, be it books, TV, music, or film. What you allow into your mind will have effects far beyond simple entertainment.

I won't dwell on how negative, depressing media can drag you down and harm you. Just rest assured that it can and it will. I'd rather talk about how *positive* media can propel you forward and inspire you. TV shows, movies, and novels that highlight triumphing over adversity, overcoming odds, redemption, and bands of people pulling together to succeed can leave you with a warm heart and a can-do spirit.

But as great as entertainment can be, the real power of media is in nonfiction self-improvement books. Putting yourself on a diet of literature that expands your mind and opens your eyes to new ways of thinking and doing things can massively improve your life. These books generally come in two varieties.

The first variety is general books that motivate and improve your communication and thinking skills, your attitude, and your leadership and management abilities (the book you're reading right now falls into this general category). Some of the classics are books that everyone should read: *Think and Grow Rich* by Napoleon Hill, *How to Win Friends and Influence People* by Dale Carnegie, and *The Power of Positive Thinking* by Norman Vincent Peale are examples of general self-improvement books that can benefit anyone. Any of these would be an excellent place to start or even read again.

The second category is books that zero in on your particular business role and career field. Encourage your salespeople to read books on sales and your managers to read books on management. All leaders can benefit from reading about topics like time management, people development skills, communication, etc. Of course, I mentioned my book *The Six Dimensions of C.H.A.N.G.E. 2.0* earlier, which addresses creating a positive change in your business. And if you're involved in any of the blue-collar industries, you definitely want to read, or reread, some of the great books written by my friends and colleagues. Just to name a few:

The Power of Positive Pricing, Matt Michel

Traction, Gino Wickman

HVAC Spells Wealth, Ron Smith

The 7 Power Contractor, Al Levi

Home Service Millionaire, Tommy Mello

Where Did the Money Go, Ellen Rohr

The E-Myth HVAC Contractor, Ken Goodrich and Michael E. Gerber

Put yourself on a regular reading program, and you'll build knowledge and skills that will dramatically increase your effectiveness and leadership ability. It's time well spent!

The Fifth M: MINDFUL INTENTION. Don't dive blindly into your day. Take time each morning (or maybe the evening before) to plan your day with *intention*. It's like an enhanced to-do list. Just as you have an agenda of concrete items that you'd like to accomplish, you should also have an agenda for your state of mind and your mood and reinforce your planning with an intention to be positive and upbeat in the face of the random challenges that life throws at you. Most people let their moods change with the wind, victims of circumstance. Intending to be in a good mood will help *keep* you in a good mood no matter what happens.

And, as I'm sure you know, moods are contagious. If you can stay in a good mood, even under stress and in the face of trouble, the people around you will stay in better moods, too. And they, in turn, will impact the moods of others. It's a good-mood chain reaction!

This brings me to an important point: the Five M's are good for everyone. Spread them around. Lead by example. Let people see you living them. A rising tide lifts all boats. It's up to you to make it happen.

A Bonus M: MISS A DAY. One last thing: take a day off. That's right—miss a day of work. Seriously. One of the limiting beliefs we've built is the idea that you can never, really and truly, take a day off. Vacations are part of most compensation packages, yet we feel guilty when taking them. How messed up is that? I'm here to tell you that it's okay. I want you to boldly and proudly take a day off. Don't think about work. Let go of the stresses that haunt you, tell your team not to call you unless the building is burning down, and *take a day off*. If you feel any lingering guilt or anxiety (I know it can be hard to let it go), remind yourself that there is no productivity booster as potent as downtime. When you get back to work, you'll be refreshed and enthusiastic, ready to jump in with both feet. You'll get twice as much done, and you'll be twice as happy doing it.

What is the one area of self-care you want to improve immediately? Meditation/prayer, movement, mind download, mental food, or mindful intention?

_____

What will it mean to you and your life when you elevate this area of self-care?

_____

_____

_____

What is the first thing you can do to get started on this life change?

_____

_____

_____

The world has taught us, and we have largely adopted a collective belief, that self-care is self-ish. Nothing is further from the truth. In fact, as you can hopefully see, I believe that self-care is actually self-*less*. If you don't take care of yourself first and foremost at the highest level, how can you possibly take care of your relationships, your business, and your finances? What happens if you don't take the time to put your phone on the charger each night or periodically throughout the week? That's right, the very battery that you count on to help you perform all the countless tasks to operate your life seamlessly and effectively ends up dead! The same is true for you.

I'm often reminded of the importance of taking care of ourselves first every time I get on an airplane. They always mention the oxygen mask as they do the mandatory safety protocol explanations and demonstration. You know the one. Regardless of airline, or destination, the message is basically the same.

"Should the cabin lose pressure, oxygen masks will drop from the overhead area. Please place the mask over your own mouth and nose before assisting others."

Why do they say that? What could possibly be wrong with helping others first?

In the case of the airplane, oxygen masks are deployed in situations where the oxygen level has dropped dangerously low. Without our oxygen masks, we will quickly lose consciousness. If we don't make putting on our own mask our first priority, it is very likely we will not be able to help anyone. The same is true in every aspect of self-care! We must tend to our own needs first.

Taking care of yourself is the first step in taking care of everything else. Make it a priority, and your whole world will improve.

If my own experience will help you, please visit *www.BlueCollarBook.com* for a video training regarding my own personal daily success ritual.

CHAPTER 11

IMPLEMENTING THE 7 LAWS

IT'S BEEN SAID THAT there is no magic pill, no silver bullet, no simple way to execute the changes discussed in this book. In a sense, this is true. You can't just snap your fingers, lean back in your recliner, and expect things to happen. You have to make the effort. Knowing what to do isn't enough. You have to *implement* the changes.

WHERE KNOWLEDGE MEETS ACTION

I've attended a lot of seminars, and I've run a ton of them myself. They're a great way to meet new people, get some great new ideas, and enjoy an environment that's outside of our daily routine. I see many of the same faces at these events, and I take a special interest in tracking their progress over time. One gentleman shows up at every one of them. He's a great guy, very engaging, gives lots of great advice, and takes a real interest in the sessions.

He's even an active participant in numerous online forums, always providing help where it's needed and just generally being a positive, uplifting presence.

I also know someone who attends very few seminars and probably knows a lot less theory than the first gentleman does, but he knows enough. He isn't consumed by the latest ideas, and he doesn't rub shoulders with the "who's who" of the industry. Overall, he's a great deal less engaged in the larger business community than the first person is and, if you asked him for advice, he might shrink back and say that there are people who know a lot more about this stuff than he does. And he's probably right.

But that guy understands something that many people never quite grasp, the final, most important lesson that everything hinges on and without which everything else will fail. The first person, the one who attends all the seminars and is filled with knowledge and theory, has a company that's been stagnant for years, experiencing flat growth, stuck in essentially the same place that it was a decade ago, while the second person, the one who has only a tenth of the education, has experienced astronomical business growth and continues to scale year after year. The first person failed to take to heart what the second person put into action right away: he failed to take massive action through *implementation*.

Implementation is the magic pill, the silver bullet, in the sense that it's what makes things happen and what gets things done. But you still have to do it. You have to implement the implementation, so to speak. This is the most important, most essential part of the whole process. Without it, everything else is a waste of time. And, sadly, implementation is where most people drop the ball. You can attend every industry event, listen to every industry podcast, including mine at *www.LeadershipInaNutshell.com*, and read every book out there, but without implementation, you'll never move beyond where you are right now. Don't drop the ball. Slam-dunk it. And then, to *really* win the game, you must remain in the game and pass the ball to the next player. It isn't enough for you to implement change. You have to bring your entire team along with you.

This is a good time to take a few minutes to review what we're implementing—the seven laws:

Law #1: Authentic Abundance. Eliminate scarcity thinking and embrace a bigger future.

Law #2: Relationships before Results. Your relationships with money, spirituality, others, and yourself influence every area of your life.

Law #3: Problems Hold Solutions. Every experience is an opportunity to learn, grow, and improve your life situation.

Law #4: Purpose-Guided Responsibilities. Being a leader is all about helping others become more effective by executing your own primary purpose to the best of your ability.

Law #5: Candid Communication. Communication holds the key to unlocking the greatest results possible in every area of your life.

Law #6: Aligned Accountability. An entire team executing purposeful self-accountability creates a unique advantage.

Law #7: Essential Self-Care. Take care of yourself before you take care of others so that you can take care of everything.

Skim back through these chapters. Write down each of the Blue Collar Success Laws and post them somewhere in your office. Even better, go to *www.BlueCollarBook.com* and download a PDF of the laws. Look at them daily and remind yourself to keep each principle in play every day. Each one has a specific role; none are disposable.

IT'S GAME TIME

One key to successful implementation is changing the team mindset, on a person-to-person basis, from a negative default to a positive default. We touched on this earlier, but it's worth repeating because a positive mindset will make everything else easier going forward.

A negative-default mindset is very common; we almost seem to be hardwired to assume the worst. It takes effort to see things, especially setbacks, in a positive light. One way to help your team is positive modeling: be seen as a positive force and, as corny as it sounds, a ray of sunshine. Lead by example. Moreover, make a point of explaining this to people during performance reviews or any other time that you have an opportunity for one-on-one communication. These person-to-person sessions are also a great chance to do a little entry-level cognitive-behavior programming.

Most of what we do (and don't do) is a simple matter of programming, just like a computer. We yank our hand away from a hot burner because hot burners hurt. That's programming, and while it's an extreme example, the same principle holds true with everything we do. We're programmed to behave in certain ways, some of it inborn and some of it learned, and if we want to change our results, we have to change our programming first.

The programming is simple, but it isn't always easy. Train your team to recognize and isolate negative thoughts and reactions and to immediately turn them into positive thoughts and reactions before the negativity takes root. This takes awareness and tenacity, but it's important for what's to come. We are living in a time of rapid change in the trades, and it will not be slowing down any time soon. (For a roadmap and process to help with leading and managing change, read my book *The Six Dimensions of C.H.A.N.G.E. 2.0*). As a leader, when you roll out a new policy, procedure, or technology, you probably know how popular those changes can be. *They generally aren't popular at all.* In fact, no matter how brilliant or well-meaning they may be, they're usually met with immediate resistance by frontline team members and sometimes even other managers. Don't let this happen by default to your company. Get out in front of it. Make it easy on yourself (and everyone else) by creating a culture of positive thinking as soon as you can.

Successful change starts at the top, and the best way to lead change is to lead by example. I know I've said it before, but it bears repeating. Be visible and model the change you wish to see in others. We tend to think that people aren't influenced by our behavior, but they absolutely are, even more so when you're the one in charge. If you pay attention, you'll see it happening. Your team will emulate your language, your problem-solving methods, and your overall demeanor. It will rub off on the entire organization. This comes with a great responsibility: you have to be consistent. One slip, one snap judgment, one harsh word said in the heat of the moment can do incalculable damage and erode credibility that may take years to rebuild. The key to leadership is constant and never-ending improvement. Everything you say and do (as well as the things you don't) are always being watched. Whether you like it or not, you're a performer, and you're always on stage with an audience of vendors, clients, and teammates. Inspire them. Make them applaud.

Anyone you have the ability to influence is your audience. As any public speaker will tell you, once the audience is on your side you can work miracles. When your team is on board with you, you can get them on board with your company's purpose and mission, and you will all enjoy great success together.

Live the Blue Collar Success Laws, explain them, model them, and build them into your company's culture. If you do that, you'll find that everything will run a great deal more smoothly. Now it's time to take it to another level. Get with all of your leaders and managers, educate them, and help them to embrace and model the laws as well. Make sure they understand how the laws benefit them on a *personal* level, in addition to benefiting the company and their teammates. Do this, and you will have put into use one of the greatest secrets of the world's most successful leaders: *multiplication*. When the leaders within your company are in full collaboration with your motivations and desires, you will, in effect, have unleashed a small army to help you remake the entire organization based on your vision as a leader. If you are running a company with multiple locations, it is *essential* that you master this skill. You have to know that what is being done by your team is being done the way that you desire.

Lastly, build and reinforce a sense of ownership among the team. Make it clear that it is their company, their livelihood, their future, that it represents them as much as they represent it, and that they have a very real stake in its success and future. Team members who see themselves as owners of their positions, as personally responsible for their company's success and welfare, will perform well beyond their peers in other companies. In other words, they will be able to experience the ultimate fulfillment of a successful and meaningful career in the trades.

Utilize effective training, coaching, and delegation to instill the Blue Collar Success Laws throughout your organization, and you will have built an unstoppable, life-improving profit machine that will perform beyond your wildest dreams.

WATCH FOR TRAPS AND STAY THE COURSE

This implementation plan sounds easy enough, right? It can be, but every plan runs into unexpected problems, and this one is no different. There are two obstacles that you need to be aware of as you embark on this journey. The good news is that simple awareness, recognizing them when they rear their ugly heads, will take you a long way toward overcoming them.

The first trap is fear. Fear of change, fear of asking others to change, can stifle your progress. *Do I really want to put myself through this? Do I want to explain all of this to everyone and ask them to get on board? They'll probably think I'm crazy! It's easier to just let things continue as they have been.*

These fears are common. They affect most of us when we're at the jumping-off point of any major change. When you feel them creeping up, stop and see them for what they are: your mind's natural defense mechanism against danger and failure. Consider jumping off a cliff, and you'll get the same feedback: *You might not want to do that!* Unfortunately, your mind can be a little too aggressive, protecting you from things that will take you to the next level of achievement. Luckily, our conscious minds are stronger than these automatic reactions, and we can overcome them. Power through your fears. Don't give in to them.

The second trap is *perfectionism*. *I'll never be able to do this as well as it needs to be done, so there's no point in even trying.* Again, this is a common defense mechanism that, in spite of your brain's best intentions, will only ensure that you never advance beyond wherever you are right now. Trust me: nothing gets done as well as it ought to be. Nothing is perfect, and perfection isn't likely to start with you. That's okay. Accept the fact that your execution won't be absolutely perfect, and understand that it will probably still work pretty well and that, regardless of whatever flaws there may be, everyone will still be better off at the end than they were in the beginning. And isn't that the goal after all?

Why do most plans like this fail? Because they're begun with optimistic enthusiasm and ground down by drudgery and day-to-day reality. You lose your excitement and commitment and, before long, you've lost touch with the Success Laws, and your bold plan to implement important changes has fallen by the wayside. You have to recommit *every single day*, and it won't always be easy. There will be days when you just want to give up on it all and forget about your plans and dreams. I'm not telling you this because I'm a pessimist or because I'm trying to be "realistic"; I'm telling you because it's very likely to happen, it's extremely common, and I want you to recognize it when it does. Overcome it, stick with it, and never abandon your own purpose and vision for your life and business. Be steadfast in your dedication because it's your job to keep everyone else steadfast in theirs. The Blue Collar Success Laws *will* transform your company and everyone in it, including, and especially, YOU.

Follow and subscribe to Kenny's podcast!

PODCAST: LEADERSHIP IN A NUTSHELL

Leadership life is complex, fast-paced, and can leave you questioning your sanity! Each week, join award-winning leadership master and bestselling author Kenny Chapman as he takes on critical topics in fifteen-minute (or less) segments to help you gain conscious control of thoughts, actions, and life in general.

Listen on your favorite podcast platform or at:

www.LeadershipInaNutshell.com

ACKNOWLEDGMENTS

I AM DEEPLY GRATEFUL for all of the life experiences I've been fortunate to have during my time on the planet. Not just the amazing love and joy I've experienced, but this also includes the pain, suffering, and addictions I've transcended, which were all instrumental in helping to create the best version of myself at this time. I also want to thank everyone who has come and gone in my life as well as those that are yet to appear; the relationships are what make it all worth it. Lastly, I'd like to specifically thank all the leaders of blue-collar industry businesses: you all are the most incredible people I have ever met. I am honored to serve you as a thought leader and encourage you to continue to elevate your own consciousness as you positively impact the lives of those around you.

ARE YOU A SERVICE CONTRACTOR? KENNY FOUNDED THIS COMPANY FOR YOU!

THE BLUE COLLAR SUCCESS GROUP is the premier training and business development organization for the in-home service industry in the US, Canada, and Australia. Regardless of your size, budget, or goals, we have the tools and solutions to help you reach (and exceed) your goals. Whether you simply want to add another truck or strive to be the biggest in-home service business in the country, we can help make that happen through these offerings and more:

- Weekly live training for frontline team members

- Weekly live accountability for department-specific managers

- Custom one-on-one accountability sessions for call takers, dispatchers, technicians, salespeople, and management:

    › Office Champions Academy

    › Professional Technician Academy

    › Sales Specialist Academy

    › Management Growth Academy

For more information and to access free resources, visit:

www.TheBlueCollarSuccessGroup.com

ADDITIONAL BOOKS BY THE AUTHOR

THE SIX DIMENSIONS OF C.H.A.N.G.E. 2.0

This book shares a complete and proven system for creating positive change in your business, your relationships, your health, your free time, and your *life*. Identify an area where you feel stuck or unhappy, apply *The Six Dimensions of C.H.A.N.G.E. 2.0*, and watch your dreams become reality. Stop settling for less than what you truly want. Make the change happen today!

The Six Dimensions of C.H.A.N.G.E 2.0. is available NOW at

www.KennysBooks.com

IN-HOME SALES ACCELERATION

In-Home Sales Acceleration gives you a simple system for success. It provides specific ways to deliver the "Ultimate Client Experience," increase revenue, and keep clients for life. It also includes proprietary methodologies for becoming a better salesperson and creating sustainable income growth. You will finally break through the barriers that have held you back, take control of your results, and accelerate your sales.

In-Home Sales Acceleration is available NOW at

www.KennysBooks.com

ABOUT THE AUTHOR

KENNY CHAPMAN is an award-winning international speaker, podcaster, life mastery coach, and entrepreneur. He has owned several successful companies in very diverse industries and is the founder and CEO of The Blue Collar Success Group, Inc., accelerating the success path of home service companies.

His true passion lies in his unique Life Mastery work, helping others manifest and enjoy their goals and dreams. Kenny makes his home in Scottsdale, Arizona, but travels extensively for both business and pleasure with his wife, The Lovely Christy. For upcoming events, books, audio, and video of Kenny, and to subscribe to his acclaimed leadership podcast, please visit TheBlueCollarCoach.com.

Made in the USA
Middletown, DE
24 September 2024

61357350R00085